OXFORD READINGS IN PHILOSOPHY

Series Editor G. J. Warnock

KNOWLEDGE AND BELIEF

Also published in this series

Theories of Ethics edited by Philippa Foot

Philosophical Logic edited by P. F. Strawson

The Philosophy of Mathematics edited by Jaakko Hintikka

The Philosophy of Science edited by P. H. Nidditch

The Theory of Meaning edited by G. H. R. Parkinson

Political Philosophy edited by Anthony Quinton

The Philosophy of Language edited by John R. Searle

Moral Concepts edited by Joel Feinberg

The Philosophy of Perception edited by G. J. Warnock

The Philosophy of Action edited by Alan R. White

Reference and Modality edited by Leonard Linsky

other volumes are in preparation

KNOWLEDGE
and
BELIEF

Edited by

A. PHILLIPS GRIFFITHS

OXFORD UNIVERSITY PRESS

Oxford University Press, Ely House, London W. 1

GLASGOW NEW YORK TORONTO MELBOURNE WELLINGTON
CAPE TOWN IBADAN NAIROBI DAR ES SALAAM LUSAKA ADDIS ABABA
DELHI BOMBAY CALCUTTA MADRAS KARACHI LAHORE DACCA
KUALA LUMPUR SINGAPORE HONG KONG TOKYO

ISBN 0 19 875003 X

First published 1967
Reprinted 1968, 1973

Filmset by St. Paul's Press, Malta
and printed in Great Britain
at the University Press, Oxford
by Vivian Ridler
Printer to the University

CONTENTS

INTRODUCTION

QUESTIONS such as 'What can be known?' and 'How do we know what we know?'—questions about what claims to knowledge can in principle be justified, and how they can be justified—are the province of theory of knowledge, or epistemology. Epistemology is an important and central part of philosophy, not only for those, such as Locke and Kant, for whom epistemology is a primary interest, but also for those philosophers whose primary interest is in metaphysics, or ethics, or the philosophy of science. For metaphysical doctrines tend to modify our views both about what there is to know, and how it is to be known; ethical theories require justification, and this immediately raises epistemological issues; while the philosophy of science both requires and contributes to sophistication about epistemological issues.

Philosophers are frequently found irritating because, faced with a difficult question, they tend to talk about the question rather than trying directly to answer it. This tendency must however be accepted by anyone who is willing to sacrifice excitement, amusement, or dramatic dogmatism to the careful avoidance of confusion. The variety of answers which have been given to epistemological questions suggests very strongly that these questions themselves are being asked confusedly; and before we ask what we know and how we know it, we should ask what we mean by 'knowing'. To answer *this* question is not of course to answer the substantial epistemological ones; but it is a necessary preliminary to doing so.

The collection of articles in this book is not, except in a few cases and incidentally, about epistemology; they are all concerned with the question of what knowledge, and the related notion of belief, amount to. The collection does not pretend to be exhaustive or even representative. The articles are all drawn from writers within the recent tradition of English philosophy—those mainly influenced by such philosophers as Cook Wilson, G. E. Moore, Wittgenstein, Ryle, Ayer and Austin. With the exception of the first and fourth contributions, material has been selected entirely from articles in philosophical journals, on the grounds that most of what is of value in books is readily available to the student. To avoid a false impression of the continuing argument this book should be used in conjunction with the bibliography at the end, and particular attention paid to such books as Woozley's *Theory of Knowledge*, Ayer's *Problem of Knowledge*, and Findlay's *Values and Intentions*.

The first chapter of this volume, an extract from Cook Wilson's *Statement and Inference*, appears to deny that an investigation into what knowing is, as distinct from epistemology, is a possible one. 'Our experience of knowing then being the presupposition of any enquiry we can undertake, we cannot make knowing itself a subject of enquiry in the sense of asking what knowing is. We can make knowing a subject of enquiry but not of that kind of enquiry. We can, for instance, inquire how we come to know in general, or to know in any department of knowledge'. Cook Wilson goes on to discuss how the unanalysable universal, 'knowing', can be picked out and brought clearly to view; but it will still be unanalysable and indefinable. Yet in the extract printed in this volume, and diffusedly throughout his entire work, we find at least some account of what knowing is; indeed, in the above quotation we find the implication that knowing can be characterized as an experience. Cook Wilson's account of knowledge is admirably summed up by H. H. Price on the first page of his article *Some Considerations about Belief*, and developed in the extract from Prichard's *Knowledge and Perception*. Cook Wilson, and certainly Price, are well aware that what they are talking about as the experience of knowledge is not what is always meant by the ordinary English expression 'knowledge'. To put the point in Cook Wilson's terms, the word 'knowledge' does not always name the unanalysable universal with which he is concerned. The use of the word must be explained by its primary meaning, as the name of this universal, together with its application to other cases which have an 'affinity' with it. The Cook Wilsonian sense of 'knowing' as naming this unanalysable universal is as Price puts it a 'strict and narrow' sense. The ordinary use of the word is regarded as 'lax' and 'muddled'. Both Cook Wilson and Price are well aware of the dangers of departing from ordinary language. 'Distinctions current in language can never be safely neglected', says Cook Wilson; 'The less we depart from common usage, the less we shall mislead ourselves and our readers', says Price. But in philosophy we must depart from ordinary language where it is muddled and likely to mislead; and this, Price claims, is the case with the word 'knowledge.' He suggests that we should perhaps abandon the term 'know' altogether for philosophical purposes, and instead speak of 'apprehension' (as Cook Wilson frequently does) and, what is quite different, 'reasonable assurance'. Malcolm, on the other hand, in his article 'Knowledge and Belief', suggests no revision of language, but finds nevertheless something amounting to an ambiguity which echoes Price's account: he would distinguish a 'strong' and a 'weak' sense of 'know', at least as it occurs in the expression 'I know that *p*'. Malcolm's position is criticized in the articles by Woozley and White; other criticisms of Malcolm's thesis are noted in the bibliography.

It would be wrong to make any general objection to Price's policy of revision of ordinary language, and still less any general objections to Malcolm's policy of distinguishing between different senses of some expression. It may very well be that there are very many expressions which are ambiguous and liable to mislead. Philosophers may very well want to replace them by new technical terms for their own use: no one would say that the logician's sharpening of such terms as 'imply', 'entail', or 'infer', which, whatever their provenance, have today a bewildering variety of ordinary uses, is without point. Philosophers may alternatively want to bring to light these ambiguities in the word to avoid endemic confusions, as one very reasonably might, for example, in connection with the word 'pleasure'. The question is whether such a procedure is in fact necessary in connexion with the word 'knowledge'. It may be that Price's desire to abandon the word 'know' is a consequence not of something muddled about its ordinary use but of something about the theories of Cook Wilson. Perhaps we should go on looking and not give up so soon.

Cook Wilson and Price, then, regard an examination of ordinary language as useful and suggestive, but as no more than this. And this is primarily because it is not the use of the *word* 'know' with which they are concerned, but with the *facts*: with, one might say, the states of affairs to which the words refer, rather than with the words we use to refer to them. The search in which Cook Wilson regards himself as engaged is one for 'the explanation of the nature of the thing'—not the *word*, 'knowledge', but the *thing*, knowledge. They are convinced that there is something which is very important and which is necessary to thinking, believing, and doubting, and which might be called knowing. If we object that the ordinary use of the word 'knowing' is such that what they call knowing cannot be what we ordinarily mean by knowing, then they will reply 'Be that as it may; what we are talking about is important, and if you do not want to call it knowing, call it apprehending'. But this account seems to be trying to have things both ways. If attention to ordinary language is any kind of check, rather than a mere clue, then what we say about it cannot be irrelevant. If on the other hand our aim is to find, pick out and talk about certain recondite states of affairs which are commonly ignored, it is not very clear what a close attention to ordinary language will do for us. There are no doubt many states of affairs which were once ignored (such as those concerning magnetic fields or osmosis) and which men needed to develop a technical vocabulary to talk about. In such cases, the vulgar words they appropriated to deal with such new facts, such as 'attraction', 'force', 'energy', or 'irritability', are best understood by their new use in the technical context, rather than in terms of their original use in ordinary parlance. This, indeed, suggests that the investigation Cook Wilson was engaged in was much more like physics or empirical psychology than like what we nowadays call philosophy. It would be a useless distraction at this point to discuss whether or not his investigation should be glorified, or stigmatized, with the name of philosophy. But it surely seems that there is such a thing as the investigation of the use of words, that it is not always clear that the remarks of Price or Cook Wilson or Prichard about the use of the word 'knowledge' are correct, and that it is surely a valuable prolegomenon to any kind of discussion about knowledge to try to get clear what we mean by the word.

Such a programme may seem a very modest and rather negative one. But it is some indication of its importance that once entered on it turns out to be surprisingly difficult. Part of its difficulty arises from the fact that, while we all ask such questions as 'what is meant by "knowledge"?', we are by no means agreed as to what counts as an appropriate method of answering them. Those who hold that the meaning of a word is some object or state of affairs for which it stands might want to say that—so long as the use of the word is not 'lax' or 'muddled'—to find out what the word means is to find out what the word stands for, and examine that. This however begs an important question: is the meaning of any word an object or state of affairs to which it is sometimes used to refer? Must the meaning of the word 'knowledge' be understood in the way names are perhaps understood? We can avoid begging this question by asking instead what, in virtue of the meaning of the word, is necessary for the truth of the statements in which it occurs. We may ask, not 'What does the word "knowledge" stand for?' but rather 'What must be the case if it is true that X knows that *p*?'. The investigation will then proceed by formulating what we suspect are necessary conditions for expressions of this kind being true, which we will test by seeing whether it is ever possible correctly to say that they are true when such conditions do not hold. We will proceed by examining possible counter-examples.[1]

But how do we detect possible counter-examples? Let us take a particular example. Everyone would, it would seem, agree that 'X knows that *p*' implies that *p* is true. But we might come across someone who wanted to say that there is a counter-example to this: people in the Middle Ages knew the earth was flat, but it is not true that the earth is flat. Most of us would simply reject the counter-example. Since the world is not flat, people in the Middle Ages were wrong in thinking it flat; therefore they did not know it was flat, they merely believed it was. But in rejecting the counter-example all we are doing is insisting on the necessary condition that it is supposed to test. All we have discovered is that the objector uses the word 'know' differently from the way we do, and there is nothing more to be said. But the answer to this can be that we are not trying to find out how some particular person has decided to use the word, but how the word is used in the English language. So far as a person speaks the common language, English, his use of the word is governed by rules; but there is a great difference between his being able to use the word correctly on most occasions according to these rules, and his being able to formulate these rules correctly. His incorrect formulation of these rules may lead him to make mistakes on particular occasions of the use of the word, while his use of the word in general remains that of the normal speaker of English. The enterprise of achieving a correct formulation of these rules will, therefore, be important for the avoidance of particular mistakes.

This enterprise could be regarded as an attempt to develop a theory of the meaning of the word 'know' in English: that is to say, to discover the rules for its use. This theory would be assessed in much the way that scientific theories are assessed. It would have a method of being falsified, in that hypotheses would be tested by an examination of what is normally said. A preferable theory would be one which has simplicity and completeness: which gave as simple a set of necessary conditions as possible, and at the same time accounted for as wide a range of cases as possible in which the word 'know' appears, ruling out as few uses as possible as 'parasitic' or 'abnormal'.

[1] For an account of this method applied to the concept of knowledge, see Ayer, *The Problem of Knowledge* (chapter 1, section iv).

But it may turn out that it is practically impossible to find the kind of unity among the variety of uses of the word 'know' to provide anything which looks like a theory of its use. We may find that we are limited to a piecemeal and endless examination of particular cases, and that what we say of one case cannot be generalized to cover others. This may suggest to us that the whole enterprise is mistaken; even that the idea that words in a language are given meaning by being governed by some specifiable set of rules, like rules for the use of chessmen, is a metaphysical illusion. Perhaps one should rather say that we can point to a series of clear paradigm cases of what it is to know something, and clustered around them a range of progressively differing cases in which we do actually apply the word 'knowledge' but, in a quite different context, or for a quite different purpose, with a quite different effect.

It is certainly very difficult to formulate any simple rules for the use of the word 'know', even limiting ourselves to its use in expressions of the form 'X knows that *p*', where '*p*' is something either true or false. It would be generally agreed that no expression of the form 'X knows that *p*' is true unless *p* is true. But very little else is so obvious that it can be generally agreed.

Enough of the difficulties in finding necessary conditions for the truth of 'X knows that *p*' will come to light if we limit our consideration to those cases where 'X' refers to some individual human person. We cannot, however, say that it is a necessary condition of the truth of 'X knows that *p*' that 'X' should so refer to a human person; 'X' could refer to God, or to the United Nations Secretariat, or to a cat, without strain, and to dismiss such cases summarily as metaphorical or parasitic threatens the testability and completeness of any theory we may try to formulate. For present purposes however we may limit our sights, and ask what, given that X refers to a human individual and *p* is true, has to be true of X for 'X knows that *p*' to be true.

Must X be in some particular state of mind? Now there are two possibilities here: either that he must be in some state of mind which is unique and peculiar to knowing that something is the case; or that he must be in some state of mind otherwise describable, which he might also be in when he does not know that something is the case.

The question is, first, whether someone *must*, given the meaning of the word 'know', be in a unique state of mind when it is true of him that he knows that *p*. The question is not whether he *is as a matter of fact* always in a unique state of mind when it is true of him that he knows that *p*. It would not be possible to deny, from a mere consideration of the meaning of the word 'know', that all sorts of contingent conditions will always in fact obtain when it is true of someone that he knows something: for example, that he has a certain proportion of phosphorus in his brain, that the temperature of his environment is considerably less than 1,000 degrees centigrade, that he has lungs, or that he is in some particular state of mind; but these will not be rules for the use of the word 'know'. Whatever the contingent facts, it is false to say that someone must be in a unique state of mind when he knows that *p*, in virtue of the meaning of the word 'know'. We can happily attribute knowledge to people without any consideration of whether they are in such a unique state of mind; though it might be said to this that attributing knowledge to them *is* attributing to them this unique state of mind. But there is a much deeper objection. It has already been said that if X knows that *p* is true, then *p* is true. Now if there were a state of mind unique to knowledge and logically necessary to it, it would have to follow that being in this state of mind guaranteed the truth of what was said to be known. But it is difficult to see what the state of any human individual's mind, whatever it might be, could have to do with the truth of such statements as 'The Sun is bigger than Jupiter' or 'The Pterodactyl is extinct'. But if we admit that states of mind are in no way connected with the truth of such statements, then it is possible that the state of mind can obtain whether or not what is said to be known is true; in which case the state of mind (which might then look very like belief, or certainty, or opinion) is not unique to knowing. It is perhaps because some people have wanted to say that there is such a unique state of mind, which must obtain when someone knows something, that it has been argued that only 'immediate experience' can be truly known; for it is at least plausible to claim that while such facts as those about the Sun or Pterodactyls can have no connexion with any individual's state of mind, statements about that individual's immediate experience (e.g. 'X is in pain', 'It seems to X that he is seeing red') are so connected, in that X could not be in pain or seeming to himself to see red without knowing it. But it is enough for us to observe that any satisfactory theory of what the expression 'X knows that *p*' means in English must account for such perfectly proper locutions as 'John knows that the Sun is bigger than Jupiter' as well as such (in fact questionable) locutions as 'John knows that he (John) is in pain'.

The reader should not confuse the view criticized immediately above with that of Malcolm in his article 'Knowledge and Belief'. If being in a unique state of mind were necessary to knowing, and if one were always aware of the fact that one was in this unique state of mind, then it would follow that if a man reflects on his state of mind, he knows that he knows. Malcolm may appear to be making a similar claim, but in fact his grounds are quite different. He is not saying that there is a sense (a 'strong' sense) of the verb 'know', such that it refers to a unique state of mind; it is rather that there is a sense of 'know' which when used by me in the first person implies that I cannot be mistaken, for I would allow nothing as counter-evidence, and that I can know I am using the word 'know' in this strong sense, not by inspecting a special state of mind directed to a special kind of mental object, but by reflecting on what I am prepared to say. The major point of his article is that I can use the word 'know' in its strong sense about many ordinary empirical statements as well as about certain *a priori* statements. The point might be regarded as basically an epistemological one, and the claim that there are two 'senses' of 'know' involved as incidental. However, we may still question whether we do need to speak of two senses of 'know' on these grounds, or whether we can be satisfied with distinguishing different contexts in which one and the same word is used.[1] Would we want to say, for example, that we have two different senses of the word 'owe', as used in the sentence 'You owe me money', according to whether the alleged debtor has a witnessed and notarized document or merely a verbal promise to repay? Or would we rather say that the claim that money is owed is in either case the same, but that in the former case it is differently, and more surely, backed up?

To return to our theme: are there then any other states of mind, not unique to knowledge, but which must obtain if X knows that *p*?

Must X be aware of *p*, or thinking *p*? This is clearly not so, since we speak of people knowing things even when they are asleep (I would not withdraw my remark 'President Johnson knows a lot about politics' if I discovered that he was in fact asleep when I made it). Should we say, however, more plausibly, that if X knows that *p* then at least at some time it must have occurred to X that *p*, that at least at some time he must have thought *p*? But I am prepared to say here and now that Sir John Hunt, the famous explorer, has two lungs, and that I know this. (He must have, or he could not lead such an energetic life). But I am not prepared to say that I have just discovered it, or that I have just learned it. I am not prepared to say that I did not

[1] See also Alan R. White, 'On Claiming to Know', p. 100 of the present volume.

know this yesterday. Had someone informed me yesterday that he would tell me something I did not know, and then said 'Sir John Hunt has two lungs', I should have replied 'But I do know that'. Yet I never in my life thought about Sir John's lungs until this very minute. It does not then seem that in order for it to be true that X knows that *p*, X must be thinking, or have at some time thought, '*p*'. There is an additional difficulty that even if we did think some such condition necessary, it would be a very troublesome one to formulate. What do we mean by "being aware of '*p*'", "thinking '*p*'" (as opposed to "thinking that *p*")? Does a Frenchman think 'The horse is black' when he says 'Le cheval est noir'? He thinks perhaps *that* the horse is black; but that is not the same thing. This difficulty infects attempts to formulate some less stringent condition; such as that if someone knows that *p*, he must at least 'understand' *p*, or be capable of understanding *p*. The problem here would be in specifying what sort of capabilities are involved. A man, learning what a romantic poet is and considering Shelley might say 'Of course I always really knew that Shelley was different from Pope, and indeed that he was a romantic and Pope a classicist. I just didn't have the words to say it'. Did he 'really' know all along that Shelley was a romantic poet? It may well be that knowledge is necessarily connected with understanding, but the connexion is at best very difficult to formulate.

Let us then again narrow the field of enquiry by asking 'Given that a man does understand *p*, indeed that the thought has occurred to him, and that *p* is true, what more is required if it is to be true that he knows that *p*?'

Whether it is necessary that a man should be sure that *p*, if he is to know that *p*, is discussed by Woozley in his article 'Knowing and not Knowing' in the present volume, and I shall not pursue the matter. Can we go further and say that it is possible for a man to know that *p* even where he doubts that *p*? We must be careful here to distinguish between doubting that something is the case, and feeling unsure about it. Thus the neurotic who has to get out of his bed several times a night to 'make sure' that he has locked his doors might say that while he knows perfectly well that he has locked his doors he has to keep going to look because he has an unsure feeling, a sense of anxiety, about it; but not that he really doubts that he has locked his doors. To say 'I know very well I have locked the doors, but I feel anxious about it so I'll go and look' is to reveal a state of mind that requires explanation; but to say 'I know perfectly well that I have locked the doors, but I doubt it' sounds very like a contradiction. However the appearance of contradiction may perhaps be removed if we consider what may be said not about ourselves but about others. It may be that it is possible for X to know, and to doubt, one and the same thing; but what makes him (mistakenly) doubt it also makes him (mistakenly) think he does not know it. Imagine a small boy in school who is terrorized by a brutal teacher. He may be so put off by fear that he makes mistakes or hesitates about things which he knows perfectly well. As a well-informed, conscientious, intelligent boy he really does know the answers; yet on particularly tense occasions he really does doubt that the correct answer which springs to his lips is correct.

Many will no doubt be shocked at the suggestion that it ever makes sense to say that a man knows something when he doubts it, or does not believe it, or even actively disbelieves it. It may be that reluctance to accept this suggestion springs from concentrating on a restricted class of cases of asserting that X knows that *p*, especially where X makes the assertion about himself in the present tense. But if we look at cases where the assertion is made not to claim knowledge on one's own part, but to inculpate or exculpate another, or to make an admission on one's own part, counter-examples more easily spring to mind. In the case of the terrorized boy, we might want to keep insisting that he really knows the answers in order to point out the fault of the teacher, and the injustice of the teacher's accusation of ignorance. Again, when someone refuses to believe something, we may want not to exculpate him on the grounds that he was ignorant (culpably or not) of what he refuses to believe. Thus a mother may refuse to believe that her son is feckless, irresponsible and thoroughly untrustworthy; and we may blame her for having trusted him with young children because she knew perfectly well what she refused to believe: we might, that is, refuse her the excuse of ignorance.

There is obviously some connexion between the concepts of knowledge and belief; but it does not appear to be the simple straightforward one that if X knows *p*, X believes *p*. What the connexion is it is very difficult to say; but that there is such a connexion may be seen from the difficulty of imagining circumstances which would enable us to say that people always knew what they disbelieved, and always disbelieved what they knew.

Whether or not it is necessary for X to believe that *p* if X is to be said to know that *p*, it is certainly not sufficient. It is easy to give examples of cases where someone believes something truly but cannot be said to know it. For example, a child is shown the equation

$$x + 3 = 7$$

and is told that in it the value of x is 4. He is now asked to find the value of x in each of the following equations:

(a) $x + 1 = 2$
(b) $x + 1 = 3$
(c) $x + 1 = 4$
(d) $x + 1 = 5$

In each case, he answers '4'. He has obviously completely failed to grasp the point; and we would not be prepared to say that he knew the value of x was 4 in equation (d), though he both believes it is 4 and what he believes is true.

Such cases have led people to suggest that we may speak of knowledge only where the person concerned has *evidence* for the truth of the statement known. But this clearly will not do for a considerable range of cases.[1] These are not restricted to those cases where it may be impermissible to speak of evidence at all, for example where a man might be said to know that he has toothache (he does not go to a dentist or observe himself holding his jaw to find out he has toothache, nor is his having toothache evidence for his having toothache) or to know that two plus two equals four; it applies to knowledge that one might have evidence for but does not have evidence for. A boy, aged six, may know that France is a foreign country. But he need have no evidence for this; he must, of course, have learned it at some time, but the experience of learning it is something he may not remember and hence it could not be regarded as evidence for him.

It has been suggested that the condition that X should have evidence for *p* is too narrow, and that we should widen it to include other factors by saying that X is at least justified in believing that *p*. Gettier argues, in the article reprinted in this volume, 'Is Justified True Belief Knowledge?', that this condition, together with the conditions that *p* is true and X believes that *p*, is not sufficient for saying that X knows that *p*. Is it, however, necessary?

What do we mean by saying that X is justified in believing that *p* is true? In one sense, perhaps, X is justified in believing *p* is true if in fact *p* is true. But as we have already seen, the mere fact that *p* is true and that X believes that *p* is not either a necessary or a sufficient condition of saying that X knows that *p*. Does it mean, then, that

[1] See for example White, 'On Claiming to Know', in the present volume, p. 100.

anyone in X's position would be judged reasonable if he believed that *p*? Thus for example one might say that the six-year-old boy is reasonable in believing that France is a foreign country, because he has been taught it in school, and children reasonably believe what they have been taught in school even if they do not remember that they have been taught it. But what about the following kind of case? Many women quite unreasonably jump to conclusions about their husbands, and we do not say they knew what they say about their husbands to be true even when they happen to be right by accident. But what would we say of a woman who always made seemingly unreasonable but in fact always quite accurate accusations about her husband? She takes one look at him and says 'You've been up to something', and we find that he has indeed been losing too much at the races or kissing his secretary. We would not of course be prepared to say on the evidence of only one such occasion that she knew her husband had been up to something; but if it happened often enough, we would say that while we do not know how she knows this, somehow or other she does know it. It may be that we eventually explain her knowledge by the fact that there are some subtle indications of her husband's peccadilloes (the slight flush, the barely averted eye) in his face. But she may be quite unable to point to these. She acts, in fact, just like the unreasonable women, except that she is always right. And we would surely say, given all this information, that she knows on all these occasions, including the first. Of course, after a number of such occasions the woman herself has a reasonable ground for believing that what she believes intuitively about her husband will be true: the same ground that we have. But she cannot have had this reasonable ground on the first occasion.

Can we then say that the demand of reasonableness should be on our side, so to speak, not hers? That is, that it is the person who claims knowledge on behalf of another who has reasonable grounds for expecting that the person to whom knowledge is attributed will believe truly? Not even this would seem to follow: for just as there may be women who intuitively (as it were unreasonably but correctly) believe things about their husbands, so there may be others who know intuitively which women have intuitive knowledge; and they would not then have any *grounds* for attributing this knowledge to others.

All the intuitive woman need say is not that she has reasons for saying her husband has been kissing his secretary, but that it is reasonable for her to believe this. What makes it reasonable is that her husband has, in fact, been kissing his secretary—that what she asserts about him will be true. In the same way, a person who intuitively knows which women have intuitive knowledge of their husbands' peccadilloes need not say that he has reasons for asserting that they know, but only that their assertion is reasonable, since they do in fact know—that what he asserts about them will be correct. However, he is now asserting about them what they assert about themselves, that what they believe will in fact be true. But more seems to be required than that what they believe should be true on one single occasion, as the case of the boy who says the value of *x* is 4 on every occasion, and is right only once, shows; while we can set up the case of the intuitive woman with any plausibility at all only by saying that she appears to be consistently right.

Is it then possible to state a necessary condition of the truth of 'X knows that *p*' in terms of X's being consistently right about *p*? This will not do, because X may assert *p* only once. Thus, a man might be consistently wrong in telling us about train times; but if he took the trouble to consult a printed timetable only once, and was right on that occasion, we might say that he knew the correct train time on and only on that occasion. But perhaps we can introduce the notion of consistency in the following way. The reason why we want to say that the man who only once used a timetable to find out the train time knew the train time is that, *if* he used this method consistently, he *would* be consistently right. In this case, of course, what he sees in the timetable is evidence for the time of the train; and we can say that the reason he would be consistently right in this case is because he would be judging on good evidence. But this factor cannot be generalized. We can say of the six-year-old boy that he has been taught about France, that what he has been taught about France is true, and that he tends to remember what he has been taught; so that he will be consistently right in answering a certain range of questions about France. But this does not mean that at any point he is judging on good evidence or that he is justified in believing what he believes about France. Again, we can say that the intuitive woman knows about her husband's peccadilloes because she would be consistently right in what she says about him in similar circumstances: namely, when she looks at him. But this does not mean that she is judging on any evidence, or that she could justify her belief by referring to the way he looks or anything else. What it does suggest is that the reason why we do not want to say of X that he knows *p* when he truly believes *p* 'by accident' or through a guess, is that it is not the case that over a significant range of circumstances he would be consistently right in believing what he believes. Of course, it may be that in *exactly* the same circumstances, if they were repeated, he would be right. But he may not (there may be random factors); and in any case, even if he were, this would be useless to us, because we could never determine that all factors were exactly the same. Surely one of the main reasons for wanting to know whether people know things is in order that we can rely on what they say. We are interested therefore in whether they will be consistently right in relation to some set of determinable circumstances, such as that they have consulted a timetable, been to school, looked at their husbands, etc. It is less important that these circumstances may furnish evidence or reasons for what they believe, or justify them in believing what they believe (except in so far as it is the case that, if these circumstances do furnish them with evidence, then they will in fact consistently believe what is true). This may account for our willingness to say in some circumstances that someone does not believe what he knows to be true. For we may want to insist that in relation to some set of normal circumstances, X will be consistently right about such matters; but that he is not willing to believe something of the sort, or doubts it, on the particular occasion because the circumstances are quite abnormal. This also accounts for the fact that we can talk about what people know when the people we are talking about are asleep.

Even if this suggestion were accepted, and there are many difficulties about it remaining, it would not take us very far. We have been able to hazard so much only by severely limiting the questions we have been asking. Furthermore, no attempt has been made, in finding some connexion between knowledge and belief, to examine in the same way the word 'belief'. The articles on this topic in the present volume show that there are at least as many difficulties about the concept of belief as about the concept of knowledge.

In discussing whether we can set out any necessary conditions for the truth of 'X knows that *p*', it has been assumed that in saying 'X knows that *p*' we are describing some situation or state of affairs, and we have been trying to find out what this situation or state of affairs must be if what we say is true. In the light of these difficulties, and indeed for other reasons, it may be held that 'X knows that *p*' should not be regarded as primarily a description of anything at all, and that to do so is an example of the so-called 'descriptive fallacy'. One of the most important articles on this topic, Austin's

'Other Minds', is not reprinted in the present volume, partly because of its length and partly because of its ready availability, since it has already been reprinted several times elsewhere. It is however discussed in the article by Jonathan Harrison, 'Knowing and Promising'.

I

THE RELATION OF KNOWING TO THINKING

J. COOK WILSON

THE description of logic as being some kind of investigation of thought in distinction from things may seem a safe enough generalization, yet we shall see that it involves certain difficulties. Before considering the distinction we may naturally ask for a definition of the word *thought* itself. The thought with which logic has to do seems obviously connected with knowledge, and, if we examine the normal usage of the word in English, we shall be led to the view that this connexion of thinking with knowing is a universal characteristic of the word. We shall also see that we can give no definition, in the ordinary sense of that term, either of thinking or of knowing or indeed of certain words cognate with these.

In examining the meaning of a word such as 'thought' in philosophy, we must remember that it is a term of ordinary language. It may have acquired, rightly or wrongly, some different meaning in philosophical writings and we must be careful not to confuse the two. Thus in the philosophy of Berkeley thought comes to be used in the general sense of *consciousness*. This is alien to the normal use of language; but the philosophy of Berkeley and the allied systems have come so much into vogue, that we are in danger of forgetting this and falling into confusions.[1]

Let us then first endeavour to follow actual linguistic usage and take for granted the application of the name *thinking* to certain kinds of

From *Statement and Inference* by J. Cook Wilson (Clarendon Press, 1926), Vol. I, Part I, Section II, pp. 34–47. Reprinted by permission of the Clarendon Press.

[1]So also Locke's use of the word 'idea' [a] was alien and still remains alien to the normal usage of ordinary English. And the vogue of the philosophy of Locke has popularized a confusion.

[[a]'Some immediate object of the mind which it perceives and has before it.' Epistle to Reader in *An Essay*, &c.; cf. Letter I to Stillingfleet. The word is used by Hobbes, but without emphasis, in this sense, e.g. *Logic*, i. 5, § § 8 and 9.]

consciousness and its exclusion from certain other kinds. We shall then ask what is common to the things to which the name is applied. Thinking then, in its normal use, always has something to do with knowing.

There is some knowing, viz. the process of reasoning, to which the name 'thinking' is applied without any doubt. It is true that, according to an idiom of our language, when we prove by reasoning that the angles at the base of an isosceles triangle are equal we should not be said to *think* that the angles are equal, but to *know* that they are. We might therefore vaguely suppose that perhaps the *process* of reasoning is to be called thinking and that knowing is the result of such a process. This would be a mistake; for the process of reasoning is precisely the activity of knowing, as will become obvious when we discuss inference, and here, therefore, the ordinary idiom encourages a fallacy.

Thus then there is a certain kind of knowing, which must be called thinking if anything is.

But, on the other hand, there are activities, often, at least, called knowing, which would not be called thinking. If every apprehension of the nature of an object is taken to be knowledge, then perception (or at least some perception) and the apprehension[1] of a feeling would be knowledge; yet, according to the natural usage of language, they would not be called thinking.

This is probably because we regard thinking as an *originative activity of our own* (not that we have clear ideas either of activity or of origination), whereas we regard neither our perceptions nor our apprehension of feelings as originated by ourselves. On the other hand, the comparison of feelings, or of perceptions in general, we *do* regard as thinking, because we seem to originate these processes of comparison ourselves. Thus the apprehension of relations, either of some or of all of them, is accounted thinking, and probably the apprehension of universals is similarly always taken to be thinking, as depending on acts of comparison.

If then some perception is knowing, there is some knowing, i.e. the experience of perceiving and feeling, which is not accounted thinking.

Again, as not all that might be called knowing is thinking so also not all thinking is knowing.

The formation of opinion is undoubtedly called *thinking*; but,

[1] Having a mental state, for instance a feeling, whether involving our apprehension of it or not, is not, as such, to be identified with apprehension of the state. For the mental state of desiring, e.g., is not an apprehension of desiring, nor is it any kind of apprehension.

though based on knowledge, it is not knowing. Indeed, according to the English idiom already referred to, if we say we 'think' A is B, it is understood that we are not prepared to say we 'know' A is B. We are accustomed to say 'I don't know but I *think* so'. Opinion, in fact, is a decision that something is probable and, though not a decision of knowledge, is based upon our knowledge of the evidence available.

Further, there is something still more remote than opinion from knowing which would be called thinking, viz. questioning or wondering.

When we have not got to the truth which we happen to be seeking, nor formed an opinion about it, but are wondering what is true and putting questions to ourselves about it, we should be said to be thinking. This certainly is the ordinary view, and it seems natural enough when we reflect that this wonder is the force which brings into play that thinking which is the investigation of a given problem.

In an inquiry, first comes this questioning activity when we set a problem to ourselves. This implies that we know something of a given subject but are ignorant of some aspect of it which interests us. We put to ourselves questions: our attitude is obviously not that of knowing, nor even of having an opinion, but an attitude in which we wonder what the truth is. We may find the answer by experience or some other direct apprehension: or else we may see that the facts known to us at the start necessitate certain other facts and thus reach the goal by reasoning, a form of thinking which is knowing. If we arrive in either way at the knowledge which we seek, our undecided and interrogative attitude ceases. If our data are not enough we may either remain undecided, or we may form an opinion.

That thinking has something to do with knowing may be seen also by considering the thinking which is not directed to scientific knowledge, for instance deliberation in regard to action or artistic production.

When a man is planning something he would certainly be said to be thinking. He is partly wondering and inquiring, partly learning and knowing, and partly forming opinions as to what would suit his purpose. Under this head would come the process of literary composition, the production, say, of a poem or a play. The imagination which belongs to such processes seems, as mere imagination, rightly enough not accounted thinking, though there is no thinking without imagination. Remembering again can only be called thinking because it is more than mere imagination and involves apprehension.

We have found, then, included in thinking, activities of knowing of the kind which is not experiencing, viz. reasoning, apprehension of universals, and apprehension of relations between things experienced; activities also which are not knowledge, viz. inquiring, forming opinions, wondering and deliberating.

We must now ask what is there common to these activities in virtue of which they are all called thinking.

Consider what is common to wondering and knowing. Wondering involves knowing. We know something of a given subject and we know that we do *not* know something else of it, or there would be nothing to wonder about. But wondering or questioning is not identical with this latter knowledge. Wondering presupposes the idea of knowledge and is unintelligible without it, because wondering is wondering what is true, although itself not identical with any form of knowledge nor with the desire for knowledge. Further in explanation we cannot go, for the inquiring attitude is unique, cannot be expressed in terms of anything else, is its own explanation. Similarly each of the other forms of thinking owes its existence to knowing and can only be understood through itself and through knowing. Both thinking which is not knowing and knowing which is thinking seem rightly called *activities* of consciousness[1] and of consciousness which is not the experience called perception or feeling. This, then, is what is common to them: but it is a universal which is not confined to them; for willing and desiring, which are not thinking, are also activities of consciousness. But beyond the common universal of activity of consciousness, these forms of thinking have no further differentiation of it to unify them. What does unify them is the fact that the one, thinking which is not knowing, entirely depends on the other, knowing, and is only intelligible through it. This brings us to the general answer. The unity of the activities of consciousness, called forms of thinking, is not a universal which, as a specific form of the genus activity of consciousness, would cover the whole nature of each of them, a species of which thinking would be the name and of which they would be sub-species, but lies in the relation of the forms of thinking which are not knowing to the form

[1]There is a possible acceptation of the term *consciousness* which would make it inaccurate to call all thinking an activity of consciousness. If consciousness be limited to consciousness of some *object*, wondering would not be consciousness. It involves the consciousness of objects but is not itself the consciousness of an object. But then neither would desire be consciousness, for desire is not consciousness of the object desired nor of its absence.

which is knowing. Those which are not knowing arise from the desire to know or from some other relation to knowing and are unified with knowing by a special relation, depending in each case upon its peculiar nature and *sui generis*, intelligible and only intelligible by a consideration of the particular case. This therefore is a case where the ordinary idea of definition is not applicable. Ordinary definition is a statement of the general kind (genus) to which the thing to be defined belongs and of the characteristics of the particular sort (species), that is the differentiation of the kind (genus), to which the thing to be defined belongs. Thus all species of rectilinear triangles are called by the same name in consequence of a common quality, the having three straight sides. This is what is usually called an explanation of the nature of the thing. In a given case we may ask again for a definition of the assigned genus and we may go on to similar questions about this new definition. In this process we must obviously come to something which cannot be defined, in the given sense of definition, or the process would never end. Definition, in fact, itself presupposes the ending of the process in elements which cannot be themselves defined, in so-called ultimate distinctions explicable from themselves alone. This does not leave our notions indefinite, because the nature of such undefinable universals is perfectly definite and is apprehended by us in the particular instances of them. In the case of thinking, several kinds of things are called by the same name, not because of a quality common to them but because of the manner in which they are associated in reality through the peculiar relation of one of them to the rest and the nature of their dependence upon it. The same is obviously true of far less abstract universals such as colour and sound and even of *infimae species* such as blue and red.

But now, since the other activities to which the name thinking is applied depend upon knowing and to understand them we must have the idea of knowing, it might seem that, though there cannot be a definition of thinking (as definition is ordinarily understood), we must ask for a definition of knowledge. But the genus consciousness and its species knowing are universals of the kind just characterized; no account can be given of them in terms of anything but themselves. The attempt in such cases to give any explanatory account can only result in identical statements, for we should use in our explanation the very notion we professed to explain, disguised perhaps by a change of name or by the invention of some new term, say cognition or some similar imposture. We have in fact an instance of the fallacy of asking an unreal question, a question which is such in verbal form only and to which no real questioning in thought can correspond. For there are some things which cannot be made matter of question. Indeed we cannot demand an answer to any question without presupposing that we can form an estimate of the value of the answer, that is that we are capable of knowing and that we understand what knowing means; otherwise our demand would be ridiculous. Our experience of knowing then being the presupposition of any inquiry we can undertake, we cannot make knowing itself a subject of inquiry in the sense of asking what knowing is. We can make knowing a subject of inquiry but not of that kind of inquiry. We can, for instance, inquire how we come to know in general, or to know in any department of knowledge.

In the preceding investigation we have followed actual linguistic usage. We have not disputed the application of the name *thinking* and it might seem that we could do nothing else but acquiesce in it, provided we *are* examining the meaning of a name. The meaning would be a fact, in the sense at least that the application of the word to certain things was a fact, which we simply recognize as existing. We have, for example, distinguished thinking from perception; a distinction which, in ordinary usage, has become a commonplace. It appears, for instance, in Browning's *Sordello*:

> 'Thought may take perception's place
> But hardly coexist in any case'.

Suppose now that, with some modern philosophers, we contended that perception in fact involves thought and that the ordinary distinction is incorrect. If we criticized actual usage in this way, whether rightly or not, it would seem that we were appealing to other data than usage and so not really inquiring into the meaning of a name, since that must be determined by actual usage. We would appear to correct the application of a name because of our knowledge of the nature of the thing or quality signified, a knowledge which enables us to see that that nature is not present in some object to which usage attaches it. Accordingly, such an inquiry would seem to be not an inquiry into the meaning of a name but into the nature of a thing.

On the other hand, in our supposed knowledge of the nature of the thing meant by the name, in virtue of which we criticize the application of the name, it would seem that we must have started anyhow from the datum that the word is in fact applied to the given thing or quality.

As a matter of fact, in such investigations we are sometimes examining the nature of a name and sometimes the nature of *reality* without any very clear idea of the relation of these two inquiries. In philosophy there is no denying that, however it may come about, we are interested in inquiring what we and other people really mean by certain terms, e.g. by *cause, force* or *thinking*; nor is this interest confined to philosophy. General biological theory, for instance, suffers very much because an inquiry is not undertaken into what the word *life* already means in ordinary usage and what guide there is to its meaning in the things to which people apply it.

Yet there seems to be something odd in the idea of such investigation at all. If we know English we do not inquire into the meaning of 'chair', 'blue', 'loud', or 'circle'. We are supposed to know the meaning from our use of the words. Nor should we seriously try to find out the meaning of the definition of a circle by examining various circles and asking what they had in common. Again, when we do appear actually to use such a method, as when Socrates asked 'What is Justice?', whether we think we are investigating the nature of the thing or finding out what people think it is (that is, the meaning of the name), we depend obviously upon knowing that the acts we are examining are all really 'just'. It would be no use abstracting from acts that are *not* just.

How then do we know that we have included no acts that are not just? If it is through a conception of the nature of justice, a conception by which we test particular actions, then we have already what we profess to be looking for.

It seems to remain that we can only take as data the actual application of the names: if so, we are at the mercy of usage. We cannot criticize it: even if we found in it anything apparently contradictory we should be helpless to decide. Again, what security have we that we make the right generalization and find out what people really mean? If we took a look at various ellipses, we should not be likely to find the abstraction which mathematics give as their common definition, and in a look we might see no difference to speak of between a parabola and a hyperbola. Would it not be the safest way, as it is also the easiest, to ask people who use the word *what they mean*? This would certainly be the right way in the case of the ellipses or different sections of the cone.

The solution of these difficulties, as might be anticipated, is to be found in what was said about abstraction, namely, that there is a certain *feeling* of affinity between particular cases, the nature of which we do not clearly understand and cannot formulate. This explains the paradox that we are able to criticize the data on which we seem wholly to depend. The application here of the word 'feeling' is due to a proper instinct in language, in so far as it is realized that we have not here clear apprehension (or clear *thinking*) and therefore any such definite word as *knowing* is avoided. But really, feeling is not the right name nor has ordinary speech got a name for it. There are in fact certain conditions of our consciousness which are akin to thinking, akin to apprehension in general, but are neither. We shall have occasion later to recognize their existence otherwise: we shall find, for example, a condition of consciousness which simulates judgement and opinion, but is distinctly neither. In general much difficulty is caused in logic by the attempt to express everything in terms of a clear thinking consciousness. These other conditions of consciousness are not recognized and so the phenomena which belong to them get misinterpreted. The logician here has naturally been affected by language. There is a want of terms for these conditions of consciousness; their existence is imperfectly indicated by the use of such a word as *feeling* and the impulse of the philosopher is at first simply to criticize this, because he realizes there is some confusion of thought in the employment of the word.

It is difficult to describe such conditions just because there is no proper language for it, but we can indicate their character by describing the corresponding facts of consciousness. There are certain principles which exist implicitly in our minds and actuate us in particular thoughts and actions, as is shown by their operation in our attitude to particular cases. But we realize them at first *only* in particular cases; not as definite general or universal rules, of which we are clearly conscious and by which we estimate the particular cases. On the contrary, there is no such formulation to precede the particular cases: the principle lives only in the particulars. This can be understood by means of examples. Take, for instance, the logical abstraction of the syllogism. People argue quite correctly in particular syllogisms: they see the necessity of the conclusion from the premises in a particular case; they are entirely unconscious of the general rule. Thus the abstract form of it, when first presented in logic, comes as something new, while their acquiescence in the form or principle depends on an appeal to their own consciousness in which they have been implicitly using it.

A more important example, both in itself and historically, is to be found in moral rules and definitions. It seems absurd to say that a person who is distinguished for the justice of his conduct does not know what is just, and he might be rightly indignant if you denied that he knew the meaning of justice; yet he might easily be puzzled if asked to define it. Now owing to the unity of such a principle implicit in our minds there must be an affinity in the cases where we do use the term justice. We know the just man *has* a principle, and always treat him as if he had; and yet, as we see, the principle lives for him only in its application in particular cases. Indeed, the term application itself is somewhat misleading, because it rather implies that we first have the rule consciously and then apply it, which is not the case.

This affinity finds its first expression and recognition in the appearance of a common name. Often, as in the case of justice at present before us, this name has no clear, decided, definite meaning. It corresponds only to a general consciousness of affinity which has not yet arrived at a clear understanding of itself. When we begin to feel the want of a clear notion to correspond to the name and, what is perhaps more important, when we become conscious of the need of a definite rule in action, something, in fact, to make our judgements in regard to what is just more *reliable*, how have we to go to work?

Obviously we must start from the facts of the use of a name, and shall be guided at first certainly by the name: and so far we may appear to be examining the meaning of a name. Next we have to think about the individual instances, to see what they have in common, what it is in fact that has actuated us. This seems by contrast to be the examination of a thing or reality as opposed to a name. At this stage we must take first what seems to us common in certain definite cases before us: next test what we have got by considering other instances of *our own* application of the name, other instances (more accurately) in which the principle has been working in us. Now, when thus thinking of these other instances, we may see that they do not come under the formula that we have generalized. If we feel satisfied (and it is only by thinking about the particular cases that we decide whether we are or not) that these really belong to the rule, are in fact just, we require an enlargement of our formula. The definition was too narrow.

Again, arguing from the formula itself, we see how it necessitates that certain cases should fall under it: but when we consider such cases we find that we do not in ordinary life apply the notion to them and, if in our moral consciousness we are confident that they do not accord with our principle, we have correspondingly to correct our previous generalization. This time the definition is judged to be too wide.

Observe that in every such step we rely upon the rightness of our use of the principle in particular cases; this does not mean that we are sure of ourselves in every case, but that there *are* cases at all events about which we are sure. This explains what in the Socratic attempt to find definitions would otherwise be paradoxical and inexplicable. The definition depends for its correctness on the assumption that the people who wish to find the definition know what is just already and know it in the most important way, from a practical point of view. Yet all the while they are supposed to be trying to find out what justice is; and so, with the ordinary analysis, the whole procedure seems irrational. We understand now that the people who are to be instructed by the Socratic method do know in one way, and everything depends on their knowing in that way, but there is another way in which they do not know and this it is which gives the investigation a rationale and meaning.

There is a further stage when we have, or think we have, discovered the nature of the principle which has really actuated us. We may now correct some of our applications of the name because we see that some instances do not really possess the quality which corresponds to what we now understand the principle to be. This explains how it should be possible to criticize the facts out of which we have been drawing our data.

Let us apply these general considerations to the case before us, the distinction in the normal use of language between thought and perception. When the exclusion of perception from thought is called in question we have the paradox of a challenge of data. It being understood, though not necessarily after a clear investigation, that the apprehension of universals is *thinking*, we find it contended that this apprehension is found in perception but that this fact has been overlooked. Perception in consequence has been erroneously distinguished from thinking.

But there is a simpler ground for recognizing thought in perception. We are sure that reasoning is thinking, that comparing is thinking, processes which involve both the apprehending and inquiring attitudes. That being so, these are our certain data and in these activities we recognize consciousness concerned with knowing. We recognize also that we think of such processes as originated and conducted by ourselves—originative activities we may call them. We see this operating in our view of feeling; for, though it is consciousness, we distinguish it from thinking; and again we see the distinction in our ordinary disinclination to call perception thinking because of the element in it which we seem in no way to originate; an element also which seems to be what is mainly important in the matter.

Consider a sensation and our knowledge of it. The mere having a sensation, though it is consciousness, is not knowledge and must be distinguished from apprehension. To know what a sensation is I must recognize in it a definite character which distinguishes it, e.g., from other sensations. I recognize, let us say, that it is a pain, and then again a burning, or a pricking, pain, as the case may be. But this implies comparison of pain with other sensations and other pains; and thus by the activity of comparing we go beyond the mere passive state of being pained, and this activity we are sure, *ex hypothesi*, is thinking. Thus though the sensation is not originated by us we require an originative act of consciousness to apprehend it.

The same is true of other objects of consciousness in perception, which we do not ordinarily suppose to be sensations, e.g. objects seen as extended in space. Whatever passive element there is (and we certainly do not suppose ourselves to originate the shape and colouring of things) the apprehension of the characteristics of what we perceive involves a comparison; and comparison we take to be thinking. If this is so, the knowing part of perception would after all be thinking and the distinction whereby the knowing in perception was excluded from thinking, would only be a popular inaccuracy.

Yet here we must be careful to avoid an overstatement. It is not fair to condemn the ordinary view wholly, nor is it safe: for, if we do, we may lose sight of something important behind it. Distinctions current in language can never be safely neglected. In what we ordinarily recognize as comparison we have before us two objects at least and apprehend each of them distinctly. As we should say, we are thinking of the nature of both. But, in the apprehension of the definite quality of a given sensation, we are as a rule not consciously comparing it with the quality of another sensation which we distinctly remember and so have before us. We are not concerned primarily with the qualities of other things, but only with the quality of the object before us: our interest is in *it* and not in them and the fact seems to be that we have a consciousness of it as having a quality differing from that of other objects in general, but *not* a consciousness of other objects in detail. The particular qualities then of other things being in abeyance in this way and our interest being in the distinctive quality recognized in the object, we can understand how the fact that there is a comparison comes to be overlooked and how we seem to be merely appreciating the quality of the object by itself. In short, we are really comparing but do not recognize that we are. This then shows that the comparison in this case (though obviously necessary to recognizing the quality of the object as something distinct in itself and not just to be confused with anything at all) is different from ordinary comparison, and requires special recognition.

II

THE NATURE OF BELIEVING

R. B. BRAITHWAITE

PROPOSITION, as employed in modern logical discussion, has two aspects either of which may be used for its description. There is, first, the relation in which the proposition stands to fact, that is, the truth or falsity of the proposition. And there is, secondly, the relation in which the proposition stands to a mind cognizing it. Johnson emphasizes the former relation when he introduces the proposition as 'that of which truth and falsity can be significantly predicated'; Dr. Stebbing the latter when she defines it as 'anything that is believed, disbelieved, doubted, or supposed'. In this paper I shall not discuss the problems connected with the correspondence of the proposition with fact. Nor shall I discuss the most difficult problems of philosophy—those of meaning, of the conditions and methods of using symbols significantly. I intend to discuss a comparatively minor problem upon which I think I have something worth saying—that of the analysis of the cognitive relations in which I can stand to propositions, and in particular the most practically important of them, the relation of believing.

Two of the four relations given by Dr. Stebbing I shall dismiss summarily. *Disbelief* means belief in the contradictory of the proposition, and variation in degree of disbelief means inverse variation in degree of belief of the contradictory. This is simple; but I am exceedingly doubtful as to the correct analysis of *doubt*. I suspect that, when 'I doubt a proposition *p*' does not merely mean that I consider it without either believing or disbelieving it, it means that I believed it more (or disbelieved it less) in the past than I do now. But doubt may also have essential elements of feeling. However I am pretty confident that the analysis of its cognitive side is in terms of belief and supposal.

There are three other terms used for cognitive relations to

From *Proceedings of the Aristotelian Society*, Vol. 33 (1932–3), pp. 129–46. Reprinted by courtesy of the author and the Editor of the Aristotelian Society.

propositions upon which I must comment briefly. *Knowledge* I am pretty convinced is used in several different senses; but for knowledge as applied to contingent propositions known indirectly (and, of course, most of our knowing is of this sort), it is clear to me that it is a complex notion, and that the part of it which states the cognitive relation of myself to the proposition which I know is a species of belief. To speak dogmatically, the proposition 'I indirectly know the contingent proposition *p*' may be analysed into the conjunction of three propositions: (1) *p* is true, (2) I believe *p* with a high degree of belief, and (3) this high degree of belief is justifiable or reasonable. Thus the cognitive attitude in knowledge of this sort falls under belief. *Judgement* is a term used by some logicians to denote a cognitive attitude to a proposition. It seems to me that these use the word either as a synonym for belief or for belief of more than a certain degree or for belief arrived at in a certain manner. So far as we are concerned, all these fall under belief. *Assertion* I take to mean fairly strong belief together with expression by some public symbolism.

There remains, besides belief, the attitude which Dr. Stebbing calls *supposal*. This is the relation in which I stand to a proposition when I am merely considering it without either believing it or disbelieving it. It is not often that I take up this neutral attitude towards a proposition taken by itself, but I very frequently adopt it when considering its relation to some other proposition, e.g., in the hypothetical proposition 'If *p* then *q*'. I shall not use Dr. Stebbing's word 'supposal', partly because I want a word to express a relation that may occur in belief as well, and partly because supposing is only ordinarily used in reference to the purpose of the supposing, e.g., that of discovering what propositions follow from that supposed. And I shall not use the ordinary word 'considering' because that ordinarily means a process of thought continuing in time. Instead, I shall use Johnson's expression *'entertaining in thought'*. By 'I entertain a proposition *p*', I mean to say the least possible thing about my cognitive attitude, something involving neither my believing it nor my not believing it, neither my meditating upon it nor its just having come into my mind, neither my using it in a hypothetical proposition nor my making no use of it at all. To entertain a proposition in this sense is the same thing, I think, as to understand the sentence or other symbol used to stand for it; and the study of this question I take to be the essential task of philosophy. Thus the relation of entertainment is the cognitive relation *par excellence*, and the analysis of belief that I shall give will be in terms of it.

One criticism of my method of treatment must now be met. It is that entertainment always involves belief so that it is impossible to analyse the latter in terms of the former. I do not think that it would be maintained that we never entertain a proposition without believing it, but it would be maintained that we never entertain a proposition without believing some other proposition. It would also be argued that our use of words is so bound up with our beliefs that we cannot use a word in a sentence without asserting a whole set of propositions. I think that these arguments confuse a causal necessity with a logical necessity. There are doubtless causal laws connecting my past experience with my use of the word 'chair'. There are doubtless also causal laws connecting my belief that there are five chairs in my room with my entertaining the proposition that there are six chairs in the room. Thus my entertaining this proposition causally depends upon my having beliefs. Nevertheless it seems clear to me that this dependence is not logically necessary. Even if I had previously never used any of the words in the sentence 'There are six chairs in my room', and even if I have no idea of the size of the room or the number of chairs in it, if I use the sentence significantly, I entertain the proposition (whatever it is) that I am expressing by the sentence. So I do not think that an analysis of belief in terms of entertainment is circular.

After these preliminaries I come to my proposed analysis of *belief*. And first I wish to consider belief in contingent propositions that are not known directly. I am excluding, that is, beliefs in logically necessary propositions (including the propositions of formal logic and mathematics and instances of them) and beliefs in propositions which are directly known in experience. My theory of belief, therefore, applies to most of the propositions we use in ordinary life, but not to some of those which philosophers discuss.

My thesis is that 'I believe one of these propositions *p*', where believe is used in the sense of actual belief and not of a disposition to believe, means the conjunction of the two propositions: (1) I entertain *p* (where entertainment is similarly used of an actual mental state and not of a disposition to entertain), and (2) I have a disposition to act as if *p* were true. And, similarly, 'I have a disposition to believe *p*' means both that I have a disposition to entertain *p* and that I have a disposition to act as if *p* were true. In either case the former proposition is one about my mental experience and the second one about my physical behaviour. The former is subjective or phenomenological, the second objective or behaviouristic. It is the latter proposition which on my view is the *differentia* of actual belief from actual entertainment and of dispositional belief[1] from dispositional entertainment. It is a hypothetical proposition about my present and future physical behaviour, which like all propositions about physical objects can only be known indirectly on authority or on inductive grounds. Many thinkers will admit that a tendency to action is a criterion of genuine belief: the doctrine which I am advocating states that not only is it a criterion, but it is part of the actual meaning of believing.[2]

'I have a disposition to act as if *p* were true'. What is the precise meaning of this statement? I take it to assert a relationship between four things or sets of things: (1) my present and future actions, (2) the external circumstances originating the actions, (3) the relevant internal circumstances of my body and my mind, which I will call my 'needs', and (4) the proposition itself. Thus my disposition to act as if strawberries gave me indigestion means that, under relevant external circumstances (my being offered strawberries) and my needs being to preserve my health, I shall behave in a manner appropriate to the indigestibility of strawberries, namely, I shall refuse them. Under similar external circumstances, if my need is to have indigestion

[1]Henceforward I shall ignore dispositional belief, and use entertaining and believing for actual mental processes only.

[2]The thesis of this paper was, to my knowledge, first propounded by Alexander Bain. In *The Emotions and the Will* (1859) he opens his chapter upon Belief thus: 'It will be readily admitted that the state of mind called Belief is, in many cases, a concomitant of our activity. But I mean to go farther than this, and to affirm that belief has no meaning, except in reference to our actions; the essence, or import of it is such as to place it under the region of the will. . . . An intellectual notion, or conception, is likewise indispensable to the act of believing, but no mere conception that does not directly or indirectly implicate our voluntary exertions, can ever amount to the state in question' (p. 568). And in *Mental and Moral Science* (1868) he expresses it: 'The difference between mere conceiving or imagining, with or without strong feeling, and belief, is acting, or being prepared to act, when the occasion arises' (p. 372).

But in 1872, in the third edition of *Mental and Moral Science*, Bain recanted. 'I have given what I now regard as a mistaken view of the fundamental nature of the state of Belief, namely, to refer it to the Spontaneous Activity of the System. I consider the correct view to be, that belief is a primitive disposition to follow out any sequence that has been once experienced, and to expect the result' (p. 100 of the Appendix to *Mental Science*). And in the third and fourth editions of *The Emotions and the Will* (1875 and 1899), though we are told that 'Belief is essentially related to Action, that is, volition', and that 'preparedness to act upon what we affirm is admitted on all hands to be the sole, the genuine, the unmistakable criterion of belief' (p. 505), a tendency to action is no longer asserted to be the *differentia* of belief.

Ramsey adopts the causal efficacy view of belief in order to give an account of different degrees of belief, and hence of probability. But he does not defend the view as giving an account of the difference between believing and not believing, which he thinks 'could well be held to lie in the presence or absence of introspectible feelings' (*The Foundations of Mathematics*, 1931, p. 170).

(e.g., in order to avoid some unpleasant duty), I shall accept the strawberries. And my belief that strawberries are, to me, indigestible, as distinct from my merely entertaining the proposition in thought, consists of such a disposition to action.

The psychological criticism that will be made to this thesis is that the appropriateness of an action cannot be defined except in terms of beliefs. I cannot explain what I mean by my not eating the strawberries being appropriate to their indigestibility without bringing in my belief that strawberries in general, or the strawberries offered to me in particular, are indigestible. This contention does not seem to me valid. The appropriateness of my action consists in its satisfying my needs, and the satisfaction of needs is something into which no element of belief, or indeed any mental element, need enter.[1] For I am meaning by needs more than conscious desires: I mean the instinctive tendencies (whatever these may be) which are the motive forces of my life, and it is agreed that these do not always manifest themselves directly in my conscious wishes. Satisfaction of these needs is something of which I do not despair of a naturalistic explanation, though I am unable to provide anything more definite than to talk of a state of comparative quiescence following a period of complicated activity.

Of course, vague statements like these cannot be expected to satisfy a psychologist who believes that no behaviouristic account can be given of any purposive activity, whether conscious or not. And I am not concerned to defend a general behaviourism (wherever consciousness is not involved). For this paper is essentially a philosophical one, which is only concerned incidentally with questions of philosophical psychology. I wish to maintain that there are no philosophical objections to an action view of the *differentia* of belief. I take it that the function of a philosopher when confronted with any behaviouristic theory is to examine whether it is philosophically an admissible one, and then to leave it to the working psychologist to decide whether as a naturalistic hypothesis it fits the facts of human nature. A philosopher must reject some behaviouristic theories out of hand, e.g., one professing to deny consciousness altogether or one professing to give a complete behaviouristic account of meaning; but he need not reject them all. The main object of this paper is to show that a behaviouristic

[1] I do not mean by 'action' or by 'need' something necessarily excluding mental events—actions may include acts of entertainment, and needs may include conscious desires. My point is that the appropriateness of action and the satisfaction of a need do not require belief in their analysis, and that it may be possible to analyse them purely behaviouristically.

account of what differentiates belief from entertainment will do all that a philosopher requires of it.

So I must meet the philosophical objections to my doctrine. One that will be made by many philosophers—that entertaining involves believing, so that the former cannot be defined in terms of the latter, has already been answered. The second is a theoretical objection which raises an interesting point. An act of believing, it is argued,[1] cannot differ from an act of entertaining only through having different consequences, because if it has different consequences, it must differ in some other way in order to produce the different consequences. This argument rests on the deterministic hypothesis that different events always have different causes; and if this hypothesis is rejected, the argument falls to the ground. But even assuming the deterministic hypothesis, the argument does not prove what it sets out to prove. It proves indeed that the total state of myself (including both mind and body) must be different at a moment when I am believing a proposition from what it is at a moment when I am merely entertaining it. But it does not prove that the difference must be in the act of cognition, so that there is an intrinsic difference between belief and entertainment. Indeed the only reason for thinking that there is a difference is the deterministic hypothesis itself, which may be false; so a consequence of the hypothesis cannot be part of the meaning of belief.

No arguments from determinism are relevant to the analysis of a meaning. For if we accept the deterministic hypothesis that every qualitatively different effect has a qualitatively different cause, we can only do so by admitting that in many cases the cause (or the difference in the cause) is purely hypothetical. And this hypothetical event, or hypothetical property, cannot be part of the analysis of a phenomenon if it is merely assumed in order to bring the latter under the deterministic principle. We may wish to explain a mental disposition, such as the disposition to have visual memory-images of some building once seen, by 'traces' in the brain or in the 'Unconscious'; but we cannot define having memory-images in terms of such traces, because these are hypothetical and highly doubtful, whereas there is no doubt about the reality of memory. And a similar contention will hold in our case. Whether or not there is some character of an event which causally explains the difference which believing and not merely entertaining a proposition makes to my actions, this will be of no assistance in the analysis of the nature of belief itself.

[1] First by J. S. Mill against Bain, and afterwards by Brentano and Mr. Russell.

The third philosophical objection is one which will arise in most people's minds on hearing my thesis. What about those of my beliefs that have no effect upon my actions whatever? The first answer is to emphasize that my *differentia* of belief is not a set of actual actions, but a set of dispositions to action, dispositions which will not be actualized except in suitable circumstances. All that is asserted in asserting the disposition is that, if certain things happen, certain actions will take place. Nothing is asserted about what actions will take place if these things do not happen. It may perfectly well be true both that the circumstances do not happen and that, if they did arise, a specified action would take place. Anyone who denies that this has meaning is committed, I think, to the refusal of meaning to any hypothetical proposition 'If p then q' when p is known to be false. And he would be a rash man who would do this.

But, it may be said, some of my beliefs not only have no effects upon my actions, but could have no effects upon my actions. Here we must distinguish between causal and logical impossibility. I should agree that it is not much use analysing my belief in terms of a dispositional proposition that is logically impossible. If all propositions of the form 'Under certain circumstances, I shall act as if p were true' were logically impossible, I should not be able to give any of them as part of an analysis of belief. But it is only when p itself is logically impossible that to act as if it were true is logically impossible. And we have, for the present, excluded beliefs in such propositions. As for causal impossibility, I cannot agree that it matters at all. If I die immediately after believing a proposition, it is causally impossible for me to act appropriately to the proposition. But someone can perfectly well say, in the way that is perfectly natural, 'If he had lived, he would have behaved in such-and-such a way'. And it is a proposition of this sort that is all that is required by my analysis of belief. So I do not think that the fact that there are causal laws holding in the world which prevent my doing appropriate actions affects the question, since I can always consider these laws not holding, and what I should do under these (causally impossible) circumstances.

Perhaps it might be alleged that to act appropriately to a proposition about a past event is logically impossible, since all appropriate actions would be in the past, not the future. This contention seems to me simply mistaken. Not only is it not logically impossible for my beliefs about the past to affect my action, but, in fact, they very frequently do so. Events which are in my past may have consequences which are in my future, and if I believe that the event happened I may act differently from the way in which I should act if I did not believe that the event happened. My belief that Locke was born in 1632 is just the sort of belief which it might be alleged could have no effect upon my actions. Yet it would prevent my buying an autograph letter alleged to be written by Locke, if there were strong evidence that it was written before that date; it would make me regard with suspicion the scholarship of an author asserting the contrary; and, as a matter of fact, it was partly owing to it that I travelled from Cambridge to Oxford last year to assist in a celebration of his tercentenary. And of any historical event which I believe there is some possible action of mine which would be different if I lacked the belief.

I have avoided using one reply to the historical argument which I was tempted to use, namely, that there is always one form of behaviour which depends upon my beliefs—my verbal behaviour. If I am asked when Locke was born, and wish to inform my questioner, I shall answer '1632' if I believe that he was born in 1632, and '1633' if I believe that he was born in 1633. I have avoided this reply, because it would lay me open to the rejoinder that verbal behaviour was different from other behaviour, in that it could not be satisfactorily described except in terms of belief, the belief induced in the hearer, for example. I think that this rejoinder could be met, but it would lead me into a long discussion of the nature of communication and an attempt to define public meaning (as distinct from private meaning) behaviouristically, a task which I neither wish nor feel competent to do. So I have defended my analysis by reference in all cases to behaviour which does not involve inducing or attempting to induce a belief in the proposition which I believe.

There is a minor criticism which must be met. How, it may be asked, do I explain a change in the attitude of belief which I adopt towards a proposition if belief has reference to actions which I may not perform? Quite simply: one hypothetical proposition about myself at one time is true and another is false. The position is exactly similar to change in certain physical properties. When I say that a substance is malleable, for example, I mean that if I hit it with a hammer, it will be flattened—a physical disposition of the substance. But the substance can perfectly well lose its malleability under some treatment, that is, lose one disposition and acquire another. Change here consists in a hypothetical proposition about time t_1 being true while one about another time t_2 is false.

Finally, there is the very serious epistemological objection to my doctrine. According to this, although the proposition that I entertain a proposition *p* in thought is one about my momentary experience which I can know directly, the proposition that I believe the proposition *p* consists of propositions about my future behaviour. These propositions about dispositions are hypothetical propositions, which I cannot directly know. But, it may be objected, the fact that I believe a proposition is sometimes directly known by me: for example, I believe at this minute that the pencil which I am now seeing is yellow, and I know directly that I am having this belief. To this contention I should reply that in propositions of this sort (which are the only kind in which I think it can be plausibly maintained that I know directly that I have the belief), two different propositions are involved. 'The pencil which I am now seeing is yellow' means (1) that the sense-datum which I am seeing (in the sense appropriate to sense-data) is yellow, and (2) that the physical object which I am seeing (in the sense appropriate to physical objects) is a pencil. This latter proposition is a proposition about physical objects, and though I should agree that I know indirectly that I believed it, I should deny that I have direct knowledge of my believing it. It seems to me that my belief in it consists, apart from its entertainment, in appropriate actions, e.g., in trying to write with the pencil; and that my reasons for believing that I believe it are inductive. But my relation to the first proposition stands on a different footing, since this is a proposition about my immediate experience of a sort which I have specifically excluded from consideration so far. The question of these propositions is, of course, extremely difficult, and I cannot go into the matter in detail. But I am inclined to think that there are no propositions of immediate experience, if we mean by proposition something which can be entertained without knowing whether it is true or false;[1] and that it is better to say 'I perceive the fact that a certain sense-datum is yellow' than 'I believe the proposition that a certain sense-datum is yellow'. This direct knowledge which is perception, can itself be directly known, but I am inclined to think that in neither of these kinds of knowledge is there anything that is properly to be called belief. Thus the epistemological criticism of my doctrine is met by a distinction between a state of mind which is a state

[1] The case in general for supposing that there is a proposition distinct from both the sentence and the fact, lies in the fact that we can entertain a proposition without knowing whether it is true or false. But this argument for propositions does not apply to immediate experience. Ramsey's contention that I can entertain a proposition about someone else's immediate experience without knowing its truth or falsity, would be met by saying that such a proposition is of an altogether different kind from one about my own experience.

of believing, but which is not directly known, and a state of mind which is directly known, but which is not a state of believing.

However, the epistemological objection does raise a question to which I should give some definite answer:—Granted that the knowledge I have about my beliefs is obtained indirectly, by what means is it obtained? Knowledge of the entertainment part, I should say, is obtained directly, but of the disposition-to-act part always by induction. The inductions by which I infer that I shall act in a certain way seem to me to be of three kinds: (1) A direct induction from my knowledge of my behaviour in the past to knowledge of my behaviour in the future. (2) By means of *Gedankenexperimente*: I may consider how I shall act in the future in a given situation, and infer that I shall act in the way I think I shall act. (3) By relying on my feelings: I may have a feeling of conviction towards the proposition entertained, and infer that I shall act upon it. In all these three cases, however, the argument is inductive, for the three generalizations concerned—that I shall act in the future as I acted in the past, as I think I shall act, or as I feel—can only be obtained by induction from experience: I am using different criteria for my future behaviour in the three cases—knowledge of past actions, thought-experiments, feelings of conviction—but the inference from what I am using as a criterion to the existence of the belief is in each case inductive.

This is the point to say something about the feelings of conviction which we frequently associate with our beliefs, and which have been made the *differentiæ* of belief by many philosophers. I do not wish to deny that in a great number of cases I have a feeling of conviction when I believe: indeed I think that this feeling of conviction may reasonably be used as evidence for the existence of the belief. But I seem to have a belief frequently with no feeling of conviction: I believe quite thoroughly that the sun will rise to-morrow, but experience no particular feeling attached to the proposition believed. And it seems possible to have the feeling of conviction without believing a proposition. So I cannot accept the feeling as part of the essence of belief. If we adopt the deterministic hypothesis I have mentioned above, and agree that there must be something to account for our difference of behaviour when I believe a proposition, it may be that this hypothetical something produces (under suitable conditions) a feeling of conviction as well as the actions which, on my view, make up the *differentia* of the belief. But I am convinced that belief and feeling are different, and that the latter is not part of the former although we may reasonably use it as a criterion.

Besides contingent propositions directly known, to which I have alluded, I have explicitly omitted from my analysis beliefs in logically necessary propositions. Direct knowledge of these I am pretty clear is something into which belief does not enter: my seeing that $2 + 2 = 4$ is not a believing. My attitude towards such a proposition is more like that towards a proposition about a sense-datum: I have only to understand the words to know whether the proposition is true or false. But logically necessary propositions known indirectly present a very difficult problem, since we do not see directly that they are logically necessary and, consequently, there is the possibility of considering the contradictory. I suspect that in these cases what we are really believing is not the logically necessary proposition, but is an ordinary contingent proposition. A mathematician tells me, for example, that π is a transcendental number, and I should be said to believe that proposition on his authority. But what I am really believing, I suspect, is that the proposition that he is believing when he speaks certain words is a logically necessary proposition, which is a matter of fact. And, assuming that he does not see the logical necessity of the proposition directly, but sees the correctness of the proof, the proposition he is believing is that what is proved by his proof is logically necessary, which is again a question of fact. So that the only genuine logically necessary propositions which are cognized are those which are directly seen to be logically necessary. Of what this sort of direct knowledge consists is fortunately outside the scope of my paper.

It will be seen that the sorts of propositions belief in which I have not attempted to analyse as entertainment together with a disposition to action, are exactly those in which difficulties arise in considering merely what is meant by entertaining them. Anyone meditating upon meaning and the nature of propositions is forced to admit that logically necessary propositions stand in a class by themselves, and that sentences expressing them probably mean in quite a different way from other propositions. And anyone meditating upon sense-perception is forced to admit that propositions expressing direct sense-knowledge are different from other propositions. The difference is one which I have expressed by saying that I should prefer to speak of perceiving the fact directly in such cases. Thus the special cases arising in an analysis of belief are exactly the special cases in the analysis of entertainment. And since, whatever belief is, it must include entertainment, this is a great point in favour of my view.

But it has other advantages which make it very attractive to a logician. In the first place, it enables an account to be given of what constitutes degrees of belief and a theory of probability to be constructed. Ramsey has sketched a theory, based on the assumption that disposition to action is a general criterion for belief, by which degrees of belief can be measured by a sort of generalized betting. And he propounds this as a theory of probability. I do not think that this can give the whole truth about probability, that is, an analysis of every probability-proposition we make (nor, indeed, did Ramsey think this). But I do think that it gives a satisfactory account of propositions where a definite numerical probability is attributed to a definite event or set of events, as in the probabilities we attach in games of chance. And this in itself is a great achievement.

Secondly, it opens the way to an attempt to give some explanation of what is meant by reasonable or justifiable belief where such belief is arrived at by induction. For many logicians would now agree with me that to attempt to justify induction on lines at all similar to those on which deduction is justified, is a hopeless task. The justification of a deductive inference is the knowledge that the premises entail the conclusion, that the 'If *p* then *q*', according to which the inference is made, is logically necessary. But the justification of an inductive inference cannot be such knowledge, since the 'If *p* then *q*' used in induction is never logically necessary. The heroic attempts of Mr. Keynes and Dr. Broad and the less heroic efforts of Nicod and myself to get round this difficulty by using the notion of objective probability seem to me now along the wrong lines. For they all require us to know general propositions about the world which it is clear can themselves only be reached by induction. So some quite different way must be found for explaining what is meant by an inductive argument's being justified; and this is to be found, I think, along the pragmatic lines suggested by Peirce and Ramsey. Such an explanation of 'justification' will be, to put it very vaguely, in terms of the utility of our beliefs to us; and it is obviously convenient to such a method of explanation that the essence of belief should itself be a disposition to action. To speak dogmatically, a belief in *p* consists in entertaining *p* and being disposed to act appropriately to *p*'s being true, and the reasonableness of this belief consists in the appropriate actions being useful.

A third advantage of my doctrine is that it assists in one of the most subtle problems of logic, that of the analysis of general propositions. For action appropriate to a belief in a general proposition does not present any special problems. 'I am disposed to act appropriately to every P being Q' means that, whenever I am disposed to act appropriately to a thing's being P, I am disposed to act appropriately to its being Q. And 'I am disposed to act appropriately to some P being Q' means that it is false that, whenever I am disposed to act appropriately to a thing's being P, I am disposed to act appropriately to the thing's not being Q. Both of these are, of course, themselves general propositions, but so are all statements about dispositions. There is not the circularity in analysing a belief in a general proposition in terms of a general proposition that there would be in so analysing the general proposition itself, since it is only the belief part that we are analysing.

A word should be said here about circularity. There are only two sorts of vicious circularity that occur in logic. One is to infer a proposition from premises which include itself. The other is to analyse a term in terms of itself. Neither of these forms of circularity enter into my analysis of belief, nor into Ramsey's analysis of the reasonableness of belief. Circularity would only enter if I analysed belief in terms of believing propositions, or if Ramsey analysed reasonableness in terms the reasonableness of propositions. Whereas both of us effect our analyses in terms of propositions themselves, which the analysis does not require to be believed or to be believed reasonably.

In conclusion I must state that the principal reason why I am attached to my doctrine of the nature of belief, is the clarification it seems to me to produce in thinking about propositions. Once it is realized that the logically essential element of thinking is entertaining propositions, the problem of problems in philosophy is to understand what this entertaining of propositions is, that is, to understand how sentences can mean. This problem cannot be solved on behaviouristic lines: a general doctrine of meaning cannot be given in terms of physical objects only, because the sentence asserting such an analysis would itself have to be understood. But it seems to me that it is only this entertaining a proposition or understanding a sentence that cannot have a naturalistic explanation; our other attitudes towards a proposition may be so explained. And so, as regards belief, which is practically the most important act of thought, I wish to suggest an analysis of the extra element on behaviouristic lines. Thus I hope, by eleminating a side-issue, to clear the way for a frontal attack upon *the* philosophical problem—the meaning of meaning.

III

SOME CONSIDERATIONS ABOUT BELIEF

H. H. PRICE

I PROPOSE to begin by stating what may be called a prima facie theory of Belief. It is mostly derived from Cook Wilson;[1] but not entirely, and some of the terminology which I shall adopt in expounding it is by no means what he would have approved of. I shall then discuss some difficulties in the theory, and shall end by suggesting some modifications designed to meet them.

The theory begins by distinguishing belief from knowledge. In knowledge, the mind is directly confronted with a certain fact or with a certain particular. Knowledge is by definition infallible, though of course it need not be exhaustive. But it cannot intelligibly be called true, because the alternatives *true or false* have no application to it. Nor can it be called either active or passive, despite the opinion of writers on the history of Philosophy. For even to ask the question whether it is active or passive (the question which the Rationalists are supposed to have answered in one way and the Empiricists in another and Kant in both) is to commit an absurdity, the absurdity of regarding knowledge as a causal relation.[2] Knowledge is something ultimate and not further analysable. It is simply the situation in which some entity or some fact is directly present to consciousness. The fact may of course be of the form 'that p entails q'. The knowledge is then called inferring. But it is none the less direct, though its object is in this case more complex.

Belief on the other hand is always fallible. What I believe need not be the case, however firmly I believe it, and however strong the evidence I have for it. Moreover, there is a certain *indirectness* about

From *Proceedings of the Aristotelian Society*, Vol. 35 (1934–5), pp. 229–52. Reprinted by courtesy of the author and the Editor of the Aristotelian Society.

[1] Cook Wilson, *Statement and Inference*, Part II, ch. 3.

[2] I am not saying that the philosophers of the 17th and 18th centuries themselves committed this absurdity, but only that it has been thrust upon them by writers on the history of Philosophy.

belief. When I believe truly, there is a fact which makes my belief true. But this fact is not itself present to my mind. That which is present to my mind is something else, something which in this case corresponds to or accords with a fact, but in other cases does not. (It seems to me that many critics of the Correspondence Theory of Truth fail to notice that this theory is only meant to apply to belief and not at all to knowledge. A correspondence theory of knowledge would of course be absurd.)

The distinction between knowledge and false belief is obvious. That between knowledge and true belief is sometimes denied or questioned. Perhaps the following example will make it clear. Suppose I am puzzled about something. Then I myself can *know* by introspection that I am puzzled. Another man observing my behaviour, and noticing the frown on my face and the groans that I utter, can *believe* that I am puzzled; and his belief will be true. But it is obvious that *his* relation to my puzzlement is quite different from my relation to it. I do not mean merely that I am the subject or owner of the puzzlement and he is not. What I mean is that the puzzlement is not directly present to his consciousness, whereas it *is* directly present to mine. Something is indeed present to his consciousness, whatever that something should be called: not, however, the puzzlement itself, but something else which corresponds or accords with it—something which could perfectly well have been present to his mind even if the puzzlement had not existed in me at all.

It follows that it is impossible to know and to believe the same thing at the same time. If I know that A is B, I cannot at the same time believe that A is B, and if I believe it I cannot at the same time know it; though of course I might believe it at one time and know it at another.

This consequence has sometimes, I think, been denied. It is thought by some philosophers that whenever we make a statement a peculiar sort of mental act occurs which the statement expresses. (The statement would not of course *state* that this act is occurring, but it would express it, in the sense in which a groan expresses distress or a smile expresses pleasure.) This mental act is sometimes called *asserting*. Others call it *judging*. Now sometimes one knows that which one is stating, though often one does not; consequently it will be possible on this view both to know that A is B and at the same time to assert or judge that A is B. Now some people who hold this view have chosen to use the word 'believe' as a synonym for 'judge' or 'assert'. It follows that according to them one can know that something is the case and at the same time believe it.

Now for my part I very much doubt (with Cook Wilson) whether this supposed act of asserting or judging exists at all. There is indeed the act of formulating something in words or other symbols. And one can distinguish this act of inventing a statement from the subsequent act of uttering it or writing it down. It is, however, a practical act, none the less so for being private to the doer; if you like, an artistic one. It is certainly not a cognitive act, as asserting or judging is supposed to be. Also when I know some fact there are various emotional attitudes which I might have towards it, such as astonishment or fear or distress. Perhaps there is even some one emotional attitude which I always have whenever I state some fact which I know, an attitude of respect or deference or submission to this fact. And perhaps my statement always *expresses* this emotion as well as *signifying* the fact itself. But is there any *cognitive* act or attitude expressed by the statement over and above the mere knowing? I cannot see that there is. The fact is present to my consciousness, and I fabricate a sentence or other complex symbol to signify this fact. What more is there in it than this?

However, suppose there is this cognitive act which occurs whenever I make a statement and which the statement expresses. Even so, it seems to me very unfortunate to call it *belief*. For we want the word 'belief' for something else, for that mental attitude, other than knowing and contrasted with it, which I tried to describe above: for that something which is fallible and indirect, whereas knowing is infallible and direct. And this I think is what the word belief is ordinarily used to mean. We say for instance 'I don't know that he is in Oxford, but I believe he is': whereas we never say 'I know he is in Oxford *and* I believe he is'. If anyone objects to this usage, I must ask him to find another word for this non-knowing and fallible cognitive attitude; at any rate it certainly exists and we are all very familiar with it.

We may now proceed to give a prima facie analysis of belief, having shown how it differs from knowing. First we distinguish two elements in belief: (1) the *entertaining* of a proposition, (2) the *assenting to* or *adopting of* that proposition. Before going further we must say something more about each.

With regard to (1), I am of course aware that the phrase 'to entertain a proposition' is a stumbling-block to many philosophers. I shall be asked whether I hold with Bolzano and Meinong that propositions are real entities independent of the mind, existing or subsisting in a world of their own, distinct from the world of facts. I reply that I use the phrase 'entertaining a proposition' in an entirely non-committal way, to stand for an experience which we are all perfectly familiar with. Everyone knows what it is to understand a statement, without either believing or disbelieving what is stated. For instance, we can all understand the statements 'A thunderstorm is now occurring in Siam' or 'there will be a general election in September', and we can understand them without either belief or disbelief. The understanding of such a statement is something different from merely hearing or reading the words which compose the statement: it is what I call entertaining a proposition. Or again, everyone knows what it is to think of A 'as' being B, without either believing or disbelieving that A *is* B, and without knowing that A is B or that it is not. I do not know whether Smith is or is not brushing his hair at this moment, and I neither believe that he is doing so nor disbelieve it (why should I?). But I can and do think of him 'as' brushing his hair at this moment. This situation where we think of something 'as' such and such is what I am calling entertaining a proposition. About the nature of this act and of its object (whatever names they are called by) various theories have been suggested, of which the Bolzano-Meinong theory is one, but only one. I do not intend to discuss any of these theories: not because I think the topic unimportant—it has been rightly said by a Cambridge philosopher that entertaining is 'the most mental thing that we do'—but because the differences between them are irrelevant to the problems which I do wish to discuss. Whichever of these theories we hold, these problems will still arise.

In order to make clear what was meant by the word 'entertain' I had to take this act in isolation, so to speak, and consider the case where we understand a statement or think of A as B without either belief or disbelief. But in point of fact entertaining does not as a rule occur alone. We usually take up some *further* attitude towards that which we entertain. Thus entertaining is usually an element in a more complex mental attitude. It is for instance contained in doubting, questioning, supposing; it also forms part of certain emotional attitudes, as when I hope that it will be fine tomorrow, or fear that it will rain, or am surprised at a story which I read in the newspaper. In particular, believing and disbelieving contain entertaining. It can occur without them (as we have said) but not they without it.

This brings us to the second element in our prima facie theory of belief, the element of assent or adoption. To make clear what this is, we must go back a little and consider the process which precedes the forming of a belief. We begin, according to this theory, by entertaining *several* propositions (at least two) which are mutually exclusive. Let us suppose that we have lost the cat. We entertain the propositions that the cat is in the cupboard, that it is in the coal-scuttle, that it is behind the sofa. We consider or wonder about these three propositions, and as yet we believe none of them. But presently we hear a noise from the direction of the cupboard, and forthwith we *assent to* or *adopt* the proposition that the cat is in the cupboard, and *dissent from* or *reject* the other two alternative propositions.

It is difficult to give a further account of this process of assenting. It seems to me to consist of two elements, one volitional and one emotional. On the one hand, it is analogous to choice or preference or decision;[1] and it is significant that we say 'I decided (or made up my mind) *that* A was B' as well as 'I decided (or made up my mind) to do X'. When we come out of the state of considering into the state of assent we seem as it were to be coming down on one side of the fence, or to be taking a plunge. At first we were neutral as between the alternatives. But now we have come to be in favour of one and against the rest. On the other hand, assent also has an emotional side. When we believe something, we feel a feeling of *sureness* or *confidence* with regard to it. As we say, we feel comfortable about it.

The first of these factors in assent admits of no degrees. Either we decide in favour of p and against its alternatives q and r, or we do not. We may indeed revoke our decision later; but still, at the time of its occurrence it must occur wholly or not at all. But the emotional factor may have all sorts of degrees. 'I rather think that A is B' expresses a very mild degree of confidence. 'I suppose' or 'I expect' are often used colloquially, though inaccurately, to express a slightly greater degree of it than this. 'I think' expresses still more. And 'I am sure' or 'quite sure' or 'I feel certain' express a very high degree of confidence. Perhaps the lower half of the scale might be called *opinion* and the upper half *conviction*; and the upper limit might be called *absolute conviction*.[2]

[1] Cf. Descartes' *Account of Judgement*.

[2] It will be noted that my usage differs from Cook Wilson's here. I am using belief as the generic term, of which opinion and conviction are species. He makes belief an intermediate species, more confident than opinion but less confident than conviction. Others perhaps would prefer to call *all* assent upon evidence 'opinion', and would use the word 'belief' as an inclusive term covering both assent upon evidence and the quite different state of acceptance or taking for granted which we shall discuss presently.

In the instance we took above, our assent was assent *upon evidence*; we had a *reason* for believing as we did. We assented to the proposition that the cat is in the cupboard because we heard a noise coming from that direction, and no noises from the sofa or the coal-scuttle. But what is meant by 'having evidence for a proposition p', or 'having a reason for' believing it? According to the present theory, it means (*a*) *knowing* some fact and (*b*) *knowing* that this fact makes p more probable than its alternatives. Thus, according to this theory, belief always contains knowing. And this is one of the most striking points about the theory; we shall return to it later.

In this connexion, a sharp distinction is drawn between the *reasons* for a belief and the *cause* or psychological origin of it. And it is suggested that no enquiry into the psychological origins of a belief—for instance into the wishes or emotions or habits or traditions which caused people to believe a certain proposition p, has any tendency to show either that p is true or it is false. If we wish to discover whether it is true or false, we must simply consider the reasons for and against it. The difficulty here is that having a reason is itself a kind of cause. Knowing is a psychical event, no less than wishing, and like others it can have effects. It would be clearer if we said that assent can be determined in two distinct ways: (*a*) cognitively, by the knowing of evidence in favour of the proposition assented to, (*b*) emotionally and volitionally. These two cause-factors vary independently; sometimes one predominates, and sometimes the other. But in all belief both must be present in some degree. Assent could not be entirely determined by the knowing of evidence; for at least we must be *interested* in the propositions between which the evidence is to decide, otherwise we should never consider them at all. But if this is the sole effect of the emotional and volitional factors, our belief is as rational as any belief can be.

Could there on the other hand be an entirely *ir*rational belief, where assent is entirely determined by our emotions and volitions, and not at all by the knowing of evidence? I do not think that there could. Here we have to distinguish two possible cases. Suppose, for simplicity, that there are only two alternatives, p and q. And suppose that we have a great deal of evidence for p, and very little evidence for q. Can we in spite of this assent to q, owing to our hopes or fears or wishes? It seems to me that we cannot do so directly. But we may indirectly. For the wishes, etc., may divert our attention away from the evidence for p and restrict it to the evidence for q. The other case is that in which there is no evidence at all on either side, as when we come to a fork in a road, and have no evidence as to which of the two branch-roads is the right one. Here it seems to me that assent, and therefore belief, is impossible. We can only *decide to act as if* road A was the right one. But we do not on that account believe it. For we feel no confidence about its being the right one. It is true that some philosophers have tried to identify assenting to p with deciding to act as if p was true. But it is clear from this case that we can decide to act thus without believing p at all. Not only so. We sometimes decide to act as if p was true when we *dis*believe it, or even because we disbelieve it: as when we act as if a particular scientific or archaeological theory were true in order to convince someone else that it is false.

So far we have distinguished the following four factors in the situation called 'believing p':—

(1) Entertaining p together with one or more alternative propositions q and r.
(2) Knowing a fact (or set of facts) F, which is relevant to p, q and r.
(3) Knowing that F makes p more likely than q or r, i.e. having more evidence for p than for q or r.
(4) Assenting to p; which in turn includes
 (*a*) the preferring of p to q and r;
 (*b*) the feeling a certain degree of confidence with regard to p.

An interesting consequence follows. It is obvious that any belief may be mistaken (this is indeed part of the definition of belief). However much evidence we have for a proposition, and however confident we feel about it, it may still be false. Thus, in our example above, the noise in the cupboard may have been made by a rat or a small boy, and the cat may be under the sofa after all. But must the believer himself be aware of this possibility? It seems clear that according to the above analysis he must be. For he knows that there are alternatives to p. He knows that his evidence is incomplete, i.e. that there *are* other relevant facts whose *specific nature* he does not know. And he knows that F only makes p *more likely* than q and r, but does not *prove* p, nor disprove q and r.

Yet there certainly is a state of mind which we are tempted to call belief where we are *not* aware of the possibility that we may be mistaken. This is the state which the present theory calls *taking for granted* or *acceptance*, or with Cook Wilson, *being under an impression that*. (Professor Prichard, I believe, calls it 'thinking without question'.) To refuse to call it belief may seem somewhat artificial; but it does differ in a very important way from what we have hitherto been calling belief.

The traditional example of taking for granted is as follows. We see a man walking in front of us in the street having red hair and a dark blue overcoat. Without any weighing of evidence or any consideration of alternatives we straightway jump to the conclusion that it is our friend Smith. We walk up to him and slap him on the back. And then we discover that it is not Smith at all, but a perfect stranger.

Obviously this is quite different from the case discussed before. No doubt we should apologize and say 'I am sorry, I *thought* you were Smith'. But 'thought' does not here mean 'assented upon evidence with a mild degree of confidence'. We may indeed be tempted to say, as Mr. Russell does about a similar case, that our apologetic statement is simply false; that we were not *thinking* at all, but merely behaving. And sometimes this is so. But not always. It seems necessary to distinguish between this purely behaviouristic *quasi-acceptance* (if we may call it so) and acceptance proper, where we do think, at least in one sense of that ambiguous word. In acceptance proper we do entertain the proposition 'this man is Smith', and entertaining is certainly thinking. But we do not assent to it. For assent involves preference, as we have seen, and this requires the entertaining of at least two alternatives. One prefers something to something else. But here there is no something else. No alternative occurs to our mind at all. What happens is that *we do not dissent* from the proposition. Likewise it is not that we feel a certain degree of sureness with regard to the proposition. What happens is that *we do not feel unsure*. We entertain it without any doubt or question. This differs from the state of 'suspending judgement' about a proposition. There we suppress our doubts and questions by a deliberate and often painful effort. But here no doubt or question arises in us, so we do not have to suppress it. We just surrender ourselves to the proposition in a childlike and effortless way. Accordingly we are quite unaware of the fact that the proposition may after all not be true. And if it turns out false, we feel a peculiarly disconcerting and painful shock, quite different from the mild surprise and disappointment which results from the unmasking of an ordinary false belief. It is like the shock of being suddenly waked from a dream.

Having said what acceptance is, we must now ask how it comes about. Assent as we saw is determined by two independent factors, the knowing of evidence on the one side, volitional and emotional factors on the other. Obviously volitional and emotional factors play a part in determining acceptance too. If we want to see Smith, we shall be more likely to take the stranger to be Smith.[1] (Likewise if we are afraid of seeing him.) We might, indeed, be tempted to say that acceptance is wholly determined by volition and emotion; but this cannot be right. We do not mistake a wall or an elephant for Smith, nor even a scarecrow, however much we want (or fear) to see him. We have to see or hear or touch something which resembles him fairly closely. Thus our acceptance is partly caused by a cognitive process, namely, by what is called 'association of ideas'. Only the association is not of course between 'ideas' (if indeed that word means anything); it is between two sets of characteristics—the having red hair and a blue overcoat on the one side, and the remaining Smith-characteristics on the other. This association plays the same part in acceptance as the awareness of favourable evidence played in the case of belief proper. (In the purely behaviouristic quasi-acceptance the association is replaced by a conditioned reflex, connecting a certain kind of stimulus to the sense-organs with a certain kind of bodily movement.)

But here a curious complication arises. Even in acceptance, it may seem that there is *evidence* for the accepted proposition. The association has arisen because Smith does have red hair and does habitually wear a blue overcoat. But if so, the fact that this man here is red haired and wears a blue overcoat is evidence that he is Smith (its being so is of course compatible with his being in fact somebody else: evidence is not proof). But if we have got evidence for the proposition which we accept, is there really any difference between acceptance and belief after all? To clear up this point we must distinguish between the consciousness of something which is in fact evidence, and the *using* it as evidence: for instance, between perceiving something which does *in fact* make p likely and *recognizing* that it makes p likely. It is this recognizing or using which is absent in acceptance and present in belief proper. We can convince ourselves by introspection that it is absent, and we can also produce an argument to show that it must be. For if we recognize that F makes p likely, we must also recognize that p may, after all, be false, and some alternative proposition true; and this recognition is absent in acceptance, though present in belief.

[1]Yet curiously enough, we must not be *too* desirous (or fearful) of seeing Smith. For if we were, we should be more careful. Our anxiety would make us consider alternatives and weigh evidence, and we should have belief proper, instead of just jumping to a conclusion.

Indeed its absence is the differentia of acceptance, as we saw at first. Now according to ordinary usage we are only said to 'have' evidence for p when we *recognize* that such and such a fact makes p likely. Thus it is not true that in acceptance (or taking for granted) we have evidence for what we accept; though we could have it, if we aroused ourselves from our unquestioning state of mind, and considered critically what we are already conscious of.

We have now completed the statement of a prima facie theory of belief and of acceptance. Belief proper, the theory says, is reasoned assent to an entertained proposition; acceptance is unreasoned absence of dissent. And there are two practical analogues. There is the deciding to act as if p was true, and there is the mere acting as if p was true, from habit or possibly from instinct.

It seems to me that this theory is a plausible one, and probably it is widely held in one form or another. But there are certain difficulties in it which may oblige us to modify it in detail. I shall now proceed to discuss two of them. The first concerns the nature of the *evidence* for what we believe. The second concerns the sharp distinction drawn by the theory between *belief* and *acceptance*, or taking for granted.

The theory says that belief proper[1] is assent upon evidence. And by 'having evidence for p' it means, as we saw, *knowing* something which makes p likely. Thus belief must always contain knowledge. But if we consider instances, difficulties arise. I believe that the Emperor Galba was murdered in Rome in A.D. 69. What is my evidence for this? Does it consist of facts which I know? It certainly looks as if it consisted merely of other *believed* propositions: as that this book here is a copy of a manuscript, which in turn I believe to be a copy of a manuscript dictated or written by Tacitus; whom again I believe to have been a truthful and extremely intelligent man, able to interrogate eye-witnesses of the events which he narrates. Where are my known facts here? It seems difficult to find any; unless it be certain facts about sense-data, for instance those which I sense in looking at this book, or remember to have sensed in looking at others, or in listening to Professor X.'s lectures. Of course we say 'we know that Tacitus was a good historian' or 'we know he was alive at the time of Galba's death'. But we do not really *know* these things, if 'knowing' is used strictly, in the sense opposed to believing.

The chief difficulty of course is that in the strict sense of the word

[1] As I mentioned above, some people would call this 'opinion'.

'know' we know very little indeed. We know certain facts about sense-data and images and about our own mental processes. We know certain mathematical and logical laws. But do we in the strict sense know anything more? And there is a like difficulty about facts. What we commonly call 'the facts' in everyday speech are for the most part a set of believed propositions, namely, those which are as we say reasonably certain. Thus it is a fact, we say, that Oxford is West of Cambridge, that the earth is approximately spherical in shape, or that Queen Victoria was alive on January 1st, 1900. But although those propositions are reasonably certain, they are not *quite* certain. 'Reasonably certain' only means 'near enough to certainty', that is, so near to certainty that a reasonable man will not demand further evidence: just as 'reasonably clean' means 'so near to cleanness that a reasonable man will not demand any more soap'. It is still *possible* that any or all of these reasonably certain propositions may be false; if so, it may not after all be a fact that Oxford is West of Cambridge, for instance. And if we say we know that Oxford is West of Cambridge, as in ordinary speech we certainly should, we are using the word 'know' in a wider sense, a sense in which it is *not* contrasted with belief. It is true that even in ordinary speech we do distinguish 'knowing' from 'believing'. We say for instance 'I *believe* that Smith is still at home; I *know* that he was at home yesterday because Robinson had tea with him'. But it is painfully clear that this distinction is only one of degree. If there is 'no reasonable doubt' about a proposition, the plain man says he knows; if there is some reasonable doubt, together with a balance of favourable evidence, he says he believes.

In this situation, what is the philosopher to do? Is he to use the word 'know' in the strict and narrow sense in which Cook Wilson (for instance) uses it, to mean the having of some entity or some fact directly present to consciousness? Or shall he follow the more lax usage of ordinary speech, and mean the believing of some proposition which is reasonably certain? The second alternative may seem the more attractive. The less we depart from common usage, the less we shall mislead ourselves and our readers. But the trouble about it is that even the plain man would refuse to say 'I knew that he was at home yesterday, but now it turns out that he was not', or 'in the Middle Ages men knew that the earth was flat, but in fact it is not flat'. He would substitute some phrase like 'felt sure' or 'were convinced'. Thus common usage seems to be simply muddled on this point. On the one hand it includes under the head of knowing the firm belief in a reasonably certain proposition; on the other, it refuses to admit that knowing can be mistaken. And yet if the proposition is only reasonably certain, there is the possibility that we may be mistaken in believing it.

Perhaps the best expedient in philosophy would be to drop the word 'know' altogether. For the strict or Cook-Wilsonian sense of it we might substitute 'apprehend'[1] (as Cook Wilson himself often does). But what are we to substitute for the other sense, that in which we are said to know that the earth is approximately spherical or that Oxford is West of Cambridge? The best phrase I can think of is *reasonable assurance*. At any rate, that is the one which I propose to use in the remainder of this paper.

We may now return to the main argument. The theory which we are examining says that when we believe something p, we always have evidence for what we believe. (We must remember of course that the theory draws a sharp distinction between belief proper and mere acceptance or taking for granted.) And by having evidence it means knowing some fact or facts which make p more probable than not. We have seen reason to doubt whether belief always does contain such knowing, if the word 'know' be used in the strict sense to mean 'directly apprehend'. But it may now be suggested that at least we are always *reasonably assured* of some proposition which makes p more probable than not. Thus my evidence for believing that Galba was murdered in 69 is that I am reasonably sure that Tacitus says so and that Tacitus is a trustworthy historian.

In the majority of cases the reasonable assurance which gives us our evidence is of the sort which I have elsewhere called perceptual assurance.[2] Thus I believe that this lane leads to Little Puddlecombe. What is my evidence? That I *saw* a signpost saying so. This is perceptual assurance. But what evidence have I for believing what the signpost says? Well, on many previous occasions I have *seen* signposts saying 'To So-and-so', and later, after going in the direction indicated, have *seen* the So-and-so referred to. This is perceptual assurance again.

It is the same with our belief in any historical proposition. If history is more than coherent imagination (which according to some

[1] Some would say '*directly* apprehend'. But 'directly' is strictly speaking pleonastic.

[2] I have tried elsewhere to show that perceptual consciousness, which is to be distinguished from sensing, has two stages:-

(*a*) Perceptual Acceptance, where we just take for granted that a sense-datum belongs to some material object.

(*b*) Perceptual Assurance, where we have confirmed the existence of this object and further determined its nature by obtaining further sense-data 'confamiliar' with S.

philosophers it is not), the evidence for it must be derived from our perceptual assurance that various human beings, whom we actually see or touch or hear talking, behave in certain ways; and in particular, that part of their behaviour consists in recording other parts by means of documents and monuments. Sometimes, though rarely enough, we can directly compare the document with the things recorded in it which we remember perceiving in the past. And in many other cases what the document says is made probable by what we perceive subsequently. For instance, *The Times* says that it snowed in Derbyshire yesterday. Today I pass through Derbyshire and see some snow on the tops of the hills. Thus we have a reasonable assurance, ultimately perceptual, that many documents are veracious. And this gives us some evidence for believing that others are. Failing this perceptual evidence, I do not see that we should have the very slightest reason for believing any historical statement at all.

Now of course the far greater part of our perceptual assurance is in the past. If then it is to be available for providing evidence, it must be remembered. And is memory direct apprehension, or are we to say that it too is reasonable assurance? Or is it itself only belief upon evidence, and if so, where does the evidence come from? For a complete discussion of these questions about memory I have neither time nor capacity. Instead, I shall just offer, with apologies, a few dogmatic statements. I think we shall have to allow that there is such a thing as memory-apprehension, that is, that there are some facts about the past which we know in the strict sense of the word 'know'. And in all these facts, the remembering self is a constituent. What I apprehend is not that it rained this morning, but that this morning *I saw* it raining; not that a conference occurred at Stresa last month, but that *I read* last month that a conference was occurring. What I only believed at the time I cannot now know by memory; but I can sometimes know that I did believe it.

But of course it is not true that all memory is apprehension, or knowledge in the strict sense. Far from it. The phrase 'I remember' is a vague one, covering many different types of mental act: what is common to them is merely that they all have some reference to the past. Much of what we call memory is only belief, much is just taking for granted. Some is only the apprehending of familiar-feeling images, together with a disposition to behave in certain ways. And some is even less. Often when we are said to remember, as when I am said to remember the way to my rooms, it is only meant that on *perceiving* some material object or situation I am able to behave in certain ways; for instance on seeing the front gate of Trinity College, I can walk straight up to my rooms without even contemplating any images.

None the less some memory must be apprehension, otherwise such words as 'yesterday' would have no meaning for us at all, and so we could not even have false beliefs about the past. For it can hardly be maintained that the characteristic *having happened yesterday* is an a priori concept, or that it has been directly revealed to us by an intellectual intuition. Obviously we have become aware of it by abstraction, by examining instances; we must then have a direct apprehension of some events which are 'yesterdayish'. However, I must of course admit that memory-apprehension is fragmentary, and moreover, indeterminate or schematic. We do not now apprehend all the past events we have ever experienced, but only a few here and there; and when we do apprehend them, we apprehend only certain of their *determinable* characteristics, and not the completely *determinate* ones which they must in fact have had. Hence we tend to supplement the deficiencies of our memory apprehension by beliefs of various degrees of adequacy, and by even less reputable mental processes, such as taking for granted or the contemplation of familiar-feeling images.

If all this is correct, the fact that most of our perceptual assurances are in the past is no obstacle to the suggestion that they are what provide evidence for the vast majority of our beliefs. They occurred in the past, but we can apprehend some of them now. For instance, I can now apprehend that I have seen many signposts and have verified the information written upon them by subsequently seeing the places which they mentioned. And the same applies to any other kinds of reasonable assurance which may exist, and which may be used to provide evidence for our beliefs, when there are no known facts available (in the strict sense of 'known') or not enough, as there usually are not.

But we are now confronted with a glaring problem: what account is to be given of reasonable assurance? If it is what provides evidence for at any rate most of the propositions which we believe, is it itself in turn based upon evidence? Sometimes it clearly is. I am reasonably assured that this is a pencil. And that again is because I am reasonably assured that it is a small elongated object of hexagonal section, etc. But do I have evidence for this too? If I do, it cannot be provided by still another reasonable assurance, and the evidence for that by still another: else we have an infinite regress. But if I do not have any evidence for its being an object of that shape, etc., how is my assurance reasonable? For it is not knowing in the strict sense: I do not directly apprehend any facts about material objects at all, but only at most about sense-data. And therefore, it may be thought, my assurance needs to be justified in some way, by the production of evidence in favour of what I am assured of. And the evidence would have to be certain facts about sense-data, facts which I do directly apprehend, or know in the strict sense. Thus here at last we seem to have come upon the sort of mental process which our theory describes as believing, viz. the assenting to a proposition when we directly apprehend some facts which make the proposition more probable than not. Many of our everyday beliefs are *not* what the theory says they ought to be, for instance the belief that this lane leads to Little Puddlecombe. For there, though we do have evidence, the evidence consists not of known facts, but only of propositions which we are reasonably assured of. But it may seem that perceptual assurance itself, and perhaps other kinds of reasonable assurance, does conform to the theory very well. Let us consider whether this is really so.

On reflection it is plain that there are difficulties in admitting that perceptual assurance is belief (in the sense given to that word by our prima facie theory) or that the apprehension of sense-data provides evidence for it. Doubtless a philosopher could use various apprehended facts about sense-data as evidence for the existence of such and such a material object. At any rate many philosophers have professed to do so. And if so, *they* are believing upon evidence that such and such a material object exists. But it seems clear that their state of mind is quite different from that of the ordinary perceiving man. To put it roughly, they have got to the same conclusion as the ordinary man, but they have got there in quite a different way.

Are we to say then that the ordinary perceiving man is in a state of mere acceptance with regard to all propositions about material objects: that he merely takes for granted that there is a table here, or that he has eight fingers and two thumbs? Are we to say that he has no evidence whatever for these propositions (though a kind philosopher might provide him with some), but has merely been caused to entertain them without dissent on the occasion of sensing certain sense-data, whether by some associative process or by a mysterious kind of innate credulity? To say this would be most extravagant. There is indeed a form or stage of perceptual consciousness which is mere acceptance, as when after a single glimpse we take for granted that this is an oak tree. But perceptual assurance is something much more respectable. It arises only when we have sensed a *series* of sense-data suitably inter-related: what is at first merely accepted is thus confirmed and further specified by means of further sensings.

This brings us to the second of the two problems which I promised to discuss. When we consider perceptual assurance, it seems to be neither what our prima facie theory calls belief, nor what that theory calls acceptance. It somehow falls half-way between the two, or partakes of both. And I think it would not be hard to find other cases of this difficulty. When I say 'I am sure Smith is a truthful man', I am not necessarily expressing a mere taking for granted. And yet am I in the state which the theory calls belief? If I am, where is my evidence? The chances are that I cannot state *any* evidence at all; or if any, only very little. Perhaps I could mention one incident, or two, in which I have actually found him to be truthful; but this amount of evidence is quite disproportionate to the degree of sureness which I feel. Some candid friend may say to me, 'Very well then, you have no business to feel so sure; your sureness is just irrational'. But suppose we have met Smith a good many times, every day perhaps for several months (and the more familiar we are with him the *less* likely we are to remember particular incidents in which he was concerned); should we not all deny that our sureness was irrational? We should admit that we may be mistaken, of course. Sureness, however rational, differs fundamentally from direct apprehension, and is always fallible. But the degree of sureness which it is reasonable to feel is certainly *not* proportional to the amount of favourable evidence that one has at one's finger ends. And in some cases, we all think it perfectly reasonable to feel a very high degree of sureness when we cannot quote any evidence at all.

Nor is this confined to sureness concerning other persons. I am not claiming that we have some mysterious direct access to other minds which we do not have to material objects. The weather-wise shepherd's sureness that it will rain before night, or the motorist's sureness with regard to the capacities of his car, are equally good instances for my purpose. Neither of these men can state the evidence for his proposition, even to himself; certainly he cannot so state it as to convince an open-minded listener. The feeling of sureness has just grown up in them somehow or other. But are we going to say that this sureness is quite unreasonable, and that these men, and others whom we call 'experienced', are just taking for granted?

It may, perhaps, be suggested that in such cases we are actually knowing a number of facts which together make our proposition highly probable, but that we have not sufficient linguistic skill to state them in words, even to ourselves. Sometimes this may be so; but not always, nor even usually. It may well be that I cannot now remember *any* event which could be used as evidence to show that Smith is a truthful man. And if some one replies 'Oh! but you know many such events implicitly' I should very much like to know what he means by 'implicitly'. Philosophers try to bully us into saying that we know a number of things. And when on reflection we find that we do not, we pacify the philosophers by professing that we do know them, but only implicitly: thus having it both ways.

Perhaps before going further we ought to distinguish two cases. The first is that in which we *have* on some former occasion assented upon evidence, in the way described by our prima facie theory, though by now we have forgotten the evidence. Thus a man might once have had a lot of evidence for the proposition that the Emperor Claudius was a liberal-minded ruler. By now, after the passage of years, he has quite forgotten this evidence, but he still feels the same degree of sureness as he did. Here we should all say that his sureness is reasonable, provided he remembers that he did once have evidence, though he cannot now remember its exact nature. But the case which concerns us, the case of our sureness about Smith's truthfulness and other like cases, is different and more difficult. Here it is not that we did once assent upon evidence whose details we have now forgotten. We never assented upon evidence at all. We never considered alternative propositions, found that the facts made one more likely than the rest, and then preferred that one.

Yet it is clear that 'the general impression we have formed of him' (as we call it) is somehow derived from a multitude of experiences which we have had with regard to him. And all these things that we have experienced *might* have been used as evidence for our proposition, and we *could* therefore have assented to that proposition in the manner described by the theory. But they were not actually used so, and we never actually assented to it. Why not? Because it never occurred to us to doubt the proposition that Smith is truthful, or to consider any alternative to it. We began with a disinclination to doubt it. And the part played by those experiences was, that they progressively increased this disinclination.

Now as we should expect from our discussion of belief proper and of taking for granted, there seem to be two distinct cause-factors concerned in this increasing disinclination to doubt. One is emotional and volitional. We are disinclined to doubt a proposition when we want it to be true. And if this want increases, so does the disinclination. But we also become more and more disinclined to doubt a proposition *p when we have more and more experiences such as we should have if p were true*. If we observe Smith telling the truth on a number of particular occasions to a variety of people, we become more and more disinclined to doubt his truthfulness. We need not *notice* those events particularly, nor need we remember them. And certainly we do not say to ouselves, 'Ah! more verification of Smith's truthfulness', for then we should be using them as evidence. But our observation of them, though inattentive and unremembered, none the less has its effect upon our state of mind, and makes us less and less inclined to doubt our proposition, and less and less likely even to entertain any alternative ones. Now in so far as our disinclination to doubt is increased in *this* way, it may be called reasonable. For it is increased by a series of observations which *could* have been used as evidence, and very strong evidence, for a rational assent. And it would have been reasonable for this assent to grow more and more confident as the number of observations increased.

We now seem to have discovered what reasonable assurance is. We might define it as *a progressive disinclination to doubt an entertained proposition, where the disinclination is caused by a series of experiences which are in fact, but are not noticed to be, such as they would be if the proposition were true*. In so far as it is merely a disinclination to doubt, not a positive assent to one proposition in preference to another, it is akin to acceptance or taking for granted. Indeed what we have hitherto been calling acceptance seems to be the lower limit of it, where the disinclination is instantaneous and non-progressive and is caused by a single experience, not by an accumulating series. But in so far as the experiences which cause it *could* have been used as evidence for a confident rational assent, it is akin to belief proper, as described in our prima facie theory, and is indeed a kind of unreflective parallel or substitute for it.

It is very fortunate that there should be this progressive disinclination to doubt, which, though unreflective, is yet in a manner reasonable. There is not very much that we directly apprehend, or know in the strict sense of that word. The things which interest us most in daily life and in the natural sciences are not possible objects of immediate apprehension to such creatures as we are (perhaps angels may be more fortunate). They *are* possible subject-matters for belief, that is, for rational assent upon evidence. But we can now see that even this is a rather difficult activity, and occurs more rarely than a philosopher might suppose. We cannot always be noticing and weighing evidence, and considering alternatives. Thus it is a very good thing that in a vast number of cases where the evidence is in fact abundant and becomes progressively greater, we just slide automatically into a greater and greater disinclination to doubt as more and more observations occur.

IV

KNOWING AND BELIEVING

H. A. PRICHARD

DESCARTES could, and indeed should, have stated the reason for doubt more generally, in a way which is independent of a theological setting. He could have said that we can only have come to perceive something clearly by using such a capacity of thought as we have, i.e. our intelligence—this being necessarily so however we have acquired this capacity, i.e. whether it be due to God or not; and that consequently the doubt arises whether this capacity is equal to the task of attaining a state in which we cannot be mistaken. Therefore, he could have said, before we know anything else we must come to know that our capacity of thought is such that the use of it will give us knowledge; or, to put it otherwise, before we can know that in any particular state we cannot be mistaken and so must know some particular thing, we must first come to know that the use of our intelligence is capable of giving us knowledge. This indeed is the more general form in which the doubt presents itself to us, and in fact it was the form in which Locke presented it to himself.

The next thing to be observed is that Descartes's idea of how the doubt has to be allayed, if at all, is obviously mistaken; and we can see that it is mistaken without even considering the actual way in which Descartes considers that he allays it, viz. by discovering what he considers a *proof* that there exists a deity who is no deceiver. For as Descartes is representing the matter, such a proof could only consist in perceiving clearly and distinctly that certain things which he perceives clearly involve a necessity that such a God exists; and as precisely what he is doubtful of is whether even when he perceives something clearly and distinctly he is not mistaken, he will become doubtful, when he reflects on his having this proof, whether here, too, he is not mistaken. In exactly the same way, if we were to come to perceive clearly that our capacity of thought is competent to yield

From *Knowledge and Perception* by H. A. Prichard (Clarendon Press, 1950), pp. 85–91 and 96–97. Reprinted by permission of the Clarendon Press.

knowledge, the mere reflection that this perception is the result of our capacity would produce the very doubt about the truth of this state, which we are trying to dissipate generally. In other words, any process by which we seek to dissipate the doubt by proving it to be mistaken will itself be exposed to the very doubt which we are anxious to dissipate.

Descartes, therefore, it is obvious, is setting himself an impossible task; and we can discover it to be impossible without considering his attempt to execute it. Admitting as he does the existence of the general doubt, he would have done better to admit that it was irremovable, and that therefore even when we are certain we do not know. But if he had, he would also have had to allow that our certainty of anything could only be momentary, since on becoming certain of something we should have only to reflect on our certainty to become certain that it is not knowledge, and so to become uncertain of the thing.

Yet, as it is easy to see, there must be something wrong about Descartes's doctrine, for as we see if we reflect, we can only be uncertain of one thing because we are certain of something else, and therefore to maintain, as the sceptic does, that we are uncertain of everything is impossible.

Still what we really want to discover is what precisely is wrong with Descartes's position and what is the proper way to deal with Descartes's doubt. And to do this is not easy.

To succeed, there are two things which we absolutely must do first.

1. We must first recognize the fundamental nature of the difference between knowing and believing.

2. We must recognize that whenever we know something we either do, or at least can, by reflecting, directly know that we are knowing it, and that whenever we believe something, we similarly either do or can directly know that we are believing it and not knowing it.

As regards (1), that there is such a fundamental difference is not something which everyone will readily admit, and some will go on to the end denying it. Nevertheless, I am confident that at least the more you consider the matter the more difficult you will find it to deny the existence of the difference.

For the sake of brevity and clearness I propose to try to state dogmatically the nature of the difference, and in doing so, I shall for the most part only be trying to state Cook Wilson's view.[1] In saying that I am going to speak dogmatically I mean two things. I mean first

[1] Cook Wilson, *Statement and Inference*, Part I, chap. 11; Part II, chaps. 1,2,3.

that I am not going to offer reasons for what I am going to assert. These for the most part would from the nature of the case have to take the form of trying to meet objections; and this I propose to try to do later. I mean secondly that the statements are meant to express what I know to be *knowledge* on my part and not *opinion*, and so what is beyond controversy.

But if 'controversial' stands for any doctrine which has been disputed, then my statements will express a doctrine which is controversial, and controversial in the highest degree. Thus any of you who have had the benefit of knowing or hearing Professor J. A. Smith or Professor Joachim will realize that they would deny the truth of every statement I am going to make. But, of course, it does not follow from the mere fact that a statement is controversial in this sense that it does not express knowledge on the part of the individual who states it, and that therefore, since everything is controversial in this sense, it is useless for you to try to attain knowledge about anything.

1. Knowing is absolutely different from what is called indifferently believing or being convinced or being persuaded or having an opinion or thinking, in the sense in which we oppose thinking to knowing, as when we say 'I think so but am not sure'. Knowing is not something which differs from being convinced by a difference of degree of something such as a feeling of confidence, as being more convinced differs from being less convinced, or as a fast movement differs from a slow movement. Knowing and believing differ in kind as do desiring and feeling, or as do a red colour and a blue colour. Their difference in kind is not that of species and genus, like that of a red colour and a colour. To know is not to have a belief of a special kind, differing from beliefs of other kinds; and no improvement in a belief and no increase in the feeling of conviction which it implies will convert it into knowledge. Nor is their difference that of being two species of a common genus. It is not that there is a general kind of activity, for which the name would have to be thinking, which admits of two kinds, the better of which is knowing and the worse believing, nor is knowing something called thinking at its best, thinking not at its best being believing. Their relatedness consists rather in the facts (*a*) that believing presupposes knowing, though, of course, knowing something other than what we believe, and (*b*) that believing is a stage we sometimes reach in the endeavour to attain knowledge.

To convince ourselves of the difference between knowing and believing we need only notice that on the one hand we should only say that we know something when we are certain of it, and conversely, and that in the end we have to allow that the meaning of the terms is identical; whereas, on the other hand, when we believe something we are uncertain of it.

Further there are certain things about knowing and believing which it is essential to recognize, i.e. know, when we are considering Descartes.

(*a*) Though obviously knowledge is not false, and though obviously, when we know, we are not mistaken, knowledge is not *true*. It is neither true nor false, just as a colour is neither heavy nor light. On the other hand, beliefs are either true or false.

(*b*) Though some beliefs are true and others are false, there is no special kind of belief distinguished from others by some special characteristic such as that of being a condition of perceiving something clearly and distinctly, which, as being the kind it is, is necessarily true. Or, to put this otherwise, there is no such thing as a kind of opinion called true opinion—as Plato often implies that there is. In fact there is no sort of condition of mind of which it can truly be said that it is necessarily true; what seems nearest to this is the condition of knowing, which is necessarily not false, but yet is not true. And it may be noticed here that it is a tribute to Plato's philosophical insight, that though he considered there was a kind of opinion called true opinion, a kind which if it existed would be necessarily true, in the *Theaetetus*, where he tries to answer the question 'What is knowledge?', he will have nothing to do with the view that it is true opinion.

2. Consider the second condition, which I said must be satisfied before we can get the matter straight. We must recognize that when we know something we either do, or by reflecting can, know that our condition is one of knowing that thing, while when we believe something, we either do or can know that our condition is one of believing and not of knowing: so that we cannot mistake belief for knowledge or vice versa.

Consider instances: When knowing, for example, that the noise we are hearing is loud, we do or can know that we are knowing this and so cannot be mistaken, and when believing that the noise is due to a car we know or can know that we are believing and not knowing this. The knowledge, however, is in both cases direct; we do not know, for example, that our state is one of knowing that the noise we hear is loud indirectly, i.e. by knowing that it has some character, other than that of knowing, which we know any state must have if it is to be one of knowing—such as that of being an act of clear and distinct perceiving; we know directly that it is of the sort which knowing is; and so, too, with our knowledge that our state is one of believing.

Further, it should be noticed that in knowing that some state in which we are is one of knowing or of believing, as the case may be, we are necessarily knowing the sort of thing which knowing is and the sort of thing which believing is, even though it is impossible for us or anyone else to define either, i.e. to state its nature in terms of the nature of something else. This is obvious, because even in knowing in a given case that my condition is one of believing and not of knowing, I must be knowing the sort of thing that knowing is, since otherwise I should not know that my condition is not one of knowing, just as in knowing that some line is not straight, I must—as Plato saw—be knowing what straightness is.

Now with these two considerations in mind return to Descartes's doubt whether he was not mistaken in some past state in which he was following the proof that the angles of a triangle are equal to two right angles; and consider what we can say about it. The first thing to do is obviously to answer the question 'Was the condition of mind on which Descartes was reflecting one of knowing, or was it one of believing, or (as we say) of being convinced, as when we say we are convinced it was *X* who killed *Y*?' And, obviously, only one answer is possible. Descartes here was *knowing*; it was not a case of being *convinced*. This is something that we *know*, and to know this all we have to do is to follow the argument ourselves and then ask ourselves 'Is this condition in which, as Descartes would say, we perceive clearly for certain reasons that the angles are equal to two right angles one of *knowing*, or is it only one of being convinced?' We can only answer 'Whatever may be our state on other occasions, here we are knowing this'. And this statement is an expression of our *knowing* that we are knowing this; for we do not *believe* that we are knowing this, we know that we are.

But if that is the proper answer about Descartes's state of mind, then, of course, we know that in it he could not have been liable to deception; and therefore for ourselves we have cut off the doubt at its source. We do not require a proof of God's existence, because we know that Descartes could not have been deceived. In the same way, if his doubt had been the wider doubt whether he was not deceived because his state might have resulted from the use of an imperfect intelligence, that also is cut off for us for the same reason. For obviously a condition of knowing cannot be the result of the use of imperfect faculties.

Further, if someone were to object that after all Descartes's condition may have been liable to error, because for all we know we can later on discover some fact which is incompatible with a triangle's having angles that are equal to two right angles, we can answer that we *know* that there can be no such fact, for in knowing that a triangle must have such angles we also know that nothing can exist which is incompatible with this fact.

Further we can add: Descartes himself is just on the verge of discovering the truth when he says that *at the time*, i.e. when following the argument, he finds it impossible to believe otherwise, and finds himself saying 'Here no one can be deceiving me', and that it is only afterwards he can think that he may have been wrong. Plainly, this is just on the verge of saying 'If I consider my state at the time, I *know* that it is one of knowing'. And plainly also he afterwards only comes in fact to doubt whether even in such a state he may not have been mistaken, because he has somehow in the interval come to misrepresent to himself the character of his past state. If he had not, he could no more have doubted the truth of his state then than, as he admits, he could doubt it at the time.

And an indication that there is misrepresentation is to be found in the fact that he has to give different accounts of his state while following the demonstration, according as he describes it as it presented itself to him at the time, and as he describes it as it presented itself to him afterwards. As it presented itself at the time, he describes it as one of perceiving clearly that the angles are equal to two right angles; as it presented itself afterwards, he describes it as one in which he only *thought* he perceived clearly; and although only one of these descriptions can be true he has to introduce the second, because otherwise he could not have represented himself as afterwards doubting the truth of that state.

On Descartes's own showing, therefore, he is thinking of the state differently at the time and afterwards.

We therefore can get Descartes out of the impasse, provided we allow, *as we can*, that the state to which he referred as one of perceiving clearly was in fact one of knowing, and one which he could have known at the time to be one of knowing. By doing this we stop the rot from starting. Descartes's trouble was that he let the rot begin, and once it is allowed to start, it cannot be prevented from going on indefinitely.

I do not expect to have convinced you of the truth of all I have said. In fact I should be rather sorry if I had. For the questions which Descartes raises are far too difficult for anyone to accept statements relating to them uncritically. Probably various objections will have occurred to you, and I now propose to try to anticipate what they are and to deal with them.

The doctrine I have been either stating or implying to be true can, I think, be summarized thus:

1. We are certain of certain things, e.g. that we are wondering what is going to happen next, that we did wonder a short time ago what was going to happen next (an act of memory), that a three-sided figure is three-angled and again that the three-sidedness of a three-sided figure necessitates that the number of its angles is three, that there cannot be a test of truth.

2. To be certain of something is to know it.

3. To know something is one thing and to believe something is another.

4. When we know something, we either do or can directly know that we are knowing it, and when we believe something we know or can know that we are believing and not knowing it, and in view of the former fact, we *know* that in certain instances of its use our intelligence is not defective, so that Descartes's difficulties fall to the ground.

Now I think you will find that the objections which you may feel will reduce to two. And these are best considered separately.

The first is really only a repetition of an objection which Descartes felt to the truth of his idea that a state in which we perceive something clearly is necessarily true. It will be urged that it is preposterous to maintain that, when we are certain, we know, since obviously we and others have often been certain, and yet afterwards found that we were mistaken. Men, for example, were at one time certain that the sun goes round the earth, or that local spirits interfered with the course of nature; again two men are frequently certain of contrary things, e.g. that motion is absolute and that it is relative, that space might have a fourth dimension and that it could not, that space is infinite and that it is not. But in such cases only one can be *right*, and as both are in the same kind of state, even the one who is right cannot *know*.

In considering this objection, we should first notice that there is a state of mind which we may fail to distinguish from one of certainty, and so regard as one of certainty when it is not. This is what we may describe as an unquestioning frame of mind—or as one in which it did not occur to us to doubt something, or—as Cook Wilson described it—

one of 'being under the impression that'. I, for example, might be, as we say, thinking without question that the thing in front of me is a table, or that to-day is Tuesday, or that so and so came to see me last week. Cook Wilson said of this state that it simulates knowledge since, as is obvious, in this state there is no doubt or uncertainty. But it obviously is not the same as *being certain*. In such states we are, of course, constantly being mistaken, and unless we distinguish such states from being certain, we are apt to take instances of them as instances of our being certain and yet mistaken. And once we have noticed the distinction, we are forced to allow that we are certain of very much less than we should have said otherwise. Thus, we have to allow that we are not certain of the truth of any inductive generalization, e.g. that all men are mortal, or that sugar is sweet, for we are not *certain* that anything in the nature of a man requires that he shall at some time die; we are not even certain that the sun will rise tomorrow. And if you were asked in a law court, 'Are you certain of the truth of what you have just said?', you would probably answer, 'Well, if it comes to that there is precious little I am certain of'. It is no use to object, 'Well, if you are going to restrict what we know to what we are certain of, you are going to reduce what we know to very little'. For nothing is gained by trying to make out that we know when we do not, and the important thing is to be able to convince ourselves that there are at least some things that we know, whether the knowledge of them is important or not, especially as, if there were nothing which we knew, all our beliefs would be worthless, as having no basis in knowledge.

Next we should ask ourselves whether when we are prepared to say we know we are also prepared to say we are certain, or vice versa. Now, unquestionably, we should answer to the first question 'Yes'. For we should never think of ourselves as knowing something unless we thought of ourselves as certain. The converse, however, is not so obvious, viz. that where we should say we are certain, we should be prepared to say we know. But consider what is the alternative. If when we are certain, for example, that the square of three must be an odd number, we do not know, what *do* we do? The only possible answer is, 'In such a state we *think* we know'. But then consider what can be meant by a state of thinking we know this. The answer must be, 'Only thinking this', i.e. thinking that the square of three must be odd, as opposed to knowing that it must. But if we consider our state of mind, the retort is obvious—we do not *think* this, we *know* it. In fact, in the end it seems impossible to distinguish the meaning of knowing and being certain; any reluctance to admit this comes from a failure to distinguish being certain from what we may call thinking without question.

V

KNOWLEDGE AND BELIEF

NORMAN MALCOLM

'WE MUST recognize that when we know something we either do, or by reflecting, can know that our condition is one of knowing that thing, while when we believe something, we either do or can know that our condition is one of believing and not of knowing: so that we cannot mistake belief for knowledge or vice versa.'[1]

This remark is worthy of investigation. Can I discover *in myself* whether I know something or merely believe it?

Let us begin by studying the ordinary usage of 'know' and 'believe'. Suppose, for example, that several of us intend to go for a walk and that you propose that we walk in Cascadilla Gorge. I protest that I should like to walk beside a flowing stream and that at this season the gorge is probably dry. Consider the following cases:

(1) You say 'I believe that it won't be dry although I have no particular reason for thinking so'. If we went to the gorge and found a flowing stream we should not say that you *knew* that there would be water but that you thought so and were right.

(2) You say 'I believe that it won't be dry because it rained only three days ago and usually water flows in the gorge for at least that long after a rain'. If we found water we should be inclined to say that you knew that there would be water. It would be quite natural for you to say 'I knew that it wouldn't be dry'; and we should tolerate your remark. This case differs from the previous one in that here you had a *reason*.

(3) You say 'I know that it won't be dry' and give the same reason as in (2). If we found water we should have very little hesitation in saying that you knew. Not only had you a reason, but you *said* 'I know'

Originally published in *Mind*, Vol. 51 (1952), pp. 178–89. Reprinted in its revised form from *Knowledge and Certainty*: Essays and Lectures by Norman Malcolm, © 1963, by permission of the author and Prentice-Hall, Inc., Englewood Cliffs, New Jersey, U.S.A.

[1] H. A. Prichard, *Knowledge and Perception* (Oxford: The Clarendon Press, 1950), p. 88 [See 'Knowing and Believing', p. 61 of the present volume. Ed.]

instead of 'I believe'. It may seem to us that the latter should not make a difference—but it does.

(4) You say 'I know that it won't be dry' and give a stronger reason, e.g., 'I saw a lot of water flowing in the gorge when I passed it this morning'. If we went and found water, there would be no hesitation at all in saying that you knew. If, for example, we later met someone who said 'Weren't you surprised to see water in the gorge this afternoon?' you would reply 'No, I *knew* that there would be water; I had been there earlier in the day'. We should have no objection to this statement.

(5) Everything happens as in (4), except that upon going to the gorge we find it to be dry. We should not say that you knew, but that you *believed* that there would be water. And this is true even though you declared that you knew, and even though your evidence was the same as it was in case (4) in which you did know.

I wish to make some comments on the usage of 'know', 'knew', 'believe', and 'believed', as illustrated in the preceding cases:

(*a*) Whether we should say that you knew, depends in part on whether you had grounds for your assertion and on the strength of those grounds. There would certainly be less hesitation to say that you knew in case (4) than in case (3), and this can be due only to the difference in the strength of the grounds.

(*b*) Whether we should say that you knew, depends in part on how *confident* you were. In case (2), if you had said 'It rained only three days ago and usually water flows in the gorge for at least that long after a rain; but, of course, I don't feel absolutely sure that there will be water', then we should *not* have said that you knew that there would be water. If you lack confidence that *p* is true then others do not say that you know that *p* is true, even though *they* know that *p* is true. Being confident is a necessary condition for knowing.

(*c*) Prichard says that if we reflect we cannot mistake belief for knowledge. In case (4) you knew that there would be water, and in case (5) you merely believed it. Was there any way that you could have discovered by reflection, in case (5), that you did not know? It would have been useless to have reconsidered your grounds for saying that there would be water, because in case (4), where you *did* know, your grounds were identical. They could be at fault in (5) only if they were at fault in (4), and they were not at fault in (4). Cases (4) and (5) differ in only one respect—namely, that in one case you did subsequently find water and in the other you did not. Prichard says that we can determine by reflection whether we know something or merely believe it. But where, in these cases, is the material that reflection would strike upon? There is none.

There is only one way that Prichard could defend his position. He would have to say that in case (4) you did *not* know that there would be water. And it is obvious that he would have said this. But this is false. It is an enormously common usage of language to say, in commenting upon just such an incident as (4), 'He knew that the gorge would be dry because he had seen water flowing there that morning'. It is a usage that all of us are familiar with. We so employ 'know' and 'knew' every day of our lives. We do not think of our usage as being loose or incorrect—and it is not. As philosophers we may be surprised to observe that it *can* be that the knowledge that *p* is true should differ from the belief that *p* is true *only* in the respect that in one case *p* is true and in the other false. But that is the fact.

There is an argument that one is inclined to use as a proof that you did not know that there would be water. The argument is the following: It could have turned out that you found no water; if it had so turned out you would have been mistaken in saying that you would find water; therefore you could have been mistaken; but if you could have been mistaken then you did not know.

Now it certainly *could* have turned out that the gorge was quite dry when you went there, even though you saw lots of water flowing through it only a few hours before. This does not show, however, that you did not know that there would be water. What it shows is that *although you knew you could have been mistaken.*[1] This would seem to be a contradictory result; but it is not. It seems so because our minds are fixed upon another usage of 'know' and 'knew'; one in which 'It could have turned out that I was mistaken', implies 'I did not know'.

When is 'know' used in this sense? I believe that Prichard uses it in this sense when he says that when we go through the proof of the proposition that the angles of a triangle are equal to two right angles we *know* that the proposition is true (p. 89).[2] He says that if we put to ourselves the question: Is our condition one of knowing this, or is it only one of being convinced of it? then 'We can only answer

[1] [Some readers seem to have thought that I was denying here that 'I knew that *p*' entails 'that *p*'. That was not my intention, and my words do not have that implication. If I had said '*although you knew you were mistaken*', I should have denied the above entailment and, also, I should have misused 'knew'. The difference between the strong and weak senses of 'know' (and 'knew') is not that this entailment holds for the strong but not for the weak sense. It holds for both. If it is false that *p*, then one does not (and did not) know that *p*.]

[2] [p. 64 of the present volume. Ed.]

"Whatever may be our state on other occasions, here we are knowing this." And this statement is an expression of our *knowing* that we are knowing; for we do not *believe* that we are knowing this, we know that we are' (p. 89).[1] He goes on to say that if someone were to object that we might be making a mistake 'because for all we know we can later on discover some fact which is incompatible with a triangle's having angles that are equal to two right angles, we can answer that we *know* that there can be no such fact, for in knowing that a triangle must have such angles we also know that nothing can exist which is incompatible with this fact' (p. 90).[2]

It is easy to imagine a non-philosophical context in which it would have been natural for Prichard to have said 'I know that the angles of a triangle are equal to two right angles'. Suppose that a young man just beginning the study of geometry was in doubt as to whether that proposition is true, and had even constructed an ingenious argument that appeared to prove it false. Suppose that Prichard was unable to find any error in the argument. He might have said to the young man: 'There must be an error in it. I know that the angles of a triangle are equal to two right angles'.

When Prichard says that 'nothing can exist which is incompatible with' the truth of that proposition, is he prophesying that no one will ever have the ingenuity to construct a flawless-looking argument against it? I believe not. When Prichard says that 'we' *know* (and implies that *he* knows) that the proposition is true and *know* that nothing can exist that is incompatible with its being true, he is not making any *prediction* as to what the future will bring in the way of arguments or measurements. On the contrary, he is asserting that *nothing* that the future might bring could ever count as evidence against the proposition. He is implying that he would not *call* anything 'evidence' against it. He is using 'know' in what I shall call its 'strong' sense. 'Know' is used in this sense when a person's statement 'I know that *p* is true' implies that the person who makes the statement would look upon nothing whatever as evidence that *p* is false.

It must not be assumed that whenever 'know' is used in connexion with mathematical propositions it is used in the strong sense. A great many people have *heard* of various theorems of geometry, e.g., the Pythagorean. These theorems are a part of 'common knowledge'. If a schoolboy doing his geometry assignment felt a doubt about

[1] [p. 64 of the present volume. Ed.]

[2] [p. 65. Ed.]

the Pythagorean theorem, and said to an adult 'Are you *sure* that it is true?' the latter might reply 'Yes, I know that it is'. He might make this reply even though he could not give proof of it and even though he had never gone through a proof of it. If subsequently he was presented with a 'demonstration' that the theorem is false, or if various persons reputed to have a knowledge of geometry soberly assured him that it is false, he might be filled with doubt or even be convinced that he was mistaken. When he said 'Yes, I know that it is true', he did not pledge himself to hold to the theorem through thick and thin. He did not absolutely exclude the possibility that something could prove it to be false. I shall say that he used 'know' in the 'weak' sense.

Consider another example from mathematics of the difference between the strong and weak senses of 'know'. I have just now rapidly calculated that 92 times 16 is 1472. If I had done this in the commerce of daily life where a practical problem was at stake, and if someone had asked 'Are you sure that $92 \times 16 = 1472$?' I might have answered 'I *know* that it is; I have just now calculated it'. But also I might have answered 'I know that it is; but I will calculate it again to *make sure*'. And here my language points to a distinction. I say that I *know* that $92 \times 16 = 1472$. Yet I am willing to *confirm* it—that is, there is something that I should *call* 'making sure'; and, likewise, there is something that I should *call* 'finding out that it is false'. If I were to do this calculation again and obtain the result that $92 \times 16 = 1372$, and if I were to carefully check this latter calculation without finding any error, I should be disposed to say that I was previously mistaken when I declared that $92 \times 16 = 1472$. Thus when I say that I know that $92 \times 16 = 1472$, I allow for the possibility of a *refutation*, and so I am using 'know' in its weak sense.

Now consider propositions like $2 + 2 = 4$ and $7 + 5 = 12$. It is hard to think of circumstances in which it would be natural for me to say that I know that $2 + 2 = 4$, because no one ever questions it. Let us try to suppose, however, that someone whose intelligence I respect argues that certain developments in arithmetic have shown that $2 + 2$ does not equal 4. He writes out a proof of this in which I can find no flaw. Suppose that his demeanour showed me that he was in earnest. Suppose that several persons of normal intelligence became persuaded that his proof was correct and that $2 + 2$ does not equal 4. What would be my reaction? I should say 'I can't see what is wrong with your proof; but it *is* wrong, because I *know* that $2 + 2 = 4$'. Here I should be using 'know' in its strong sense. I should not admit that any argument or any future development in mathematics could show that it is false that $2 + 2 = 4$.

The propositions $2 + 2 = 4$ and $92 \times 16 = 1472$ do not have the same status. There *can* be a demonstration that $2 + 2 = 4$. But a demonstration would be for me (and for any average person) only a curious exercise, a sort of *game*. We have no serious interest in proving that proposition.[1] It does not *need* a proof. It stands without one, and would not fall if a proof went against it. The case is different with the proposition that $92 \times 16 = 1472$. We take an interest in the demonstration (calculation) because that proposition *depends* upon its demonstration. A calculation may lead me to reject it as false. But $2 + 2 = 4$ does *not* depend on its demonstration. It does not depend on anything! And in the calculation that proves that $92 \times 16 = 1472$, there are steps that do not depend on any calculation (e.g., $2 \times 6 = 12$; $5 + 2 = 7$; $5 + 9 = 14$).

There is a correspondence between this dualism in the logical status of mathematical propositions and the two senses of 'know'. When I use 'know' in the weak sense I am prepared to let an investigation (demonstration, calculation) determine whether the something that I claim to know is true or false. When I use 'know' in the strong sense I am not prepared to look upon anything as an *investigation*; I do not concede that anything whatsoever could prove me mistaken; I do not regard the matter as open to any *question*; I do not admit that my proposition could turn out to be false, that any future investigation *could* refute it or cast doubt on it.[2]

We have been considering the strong sense of 'know' in its application to mathematical propositions. Does it have application anywhere in the realm of *empirical* propositions—for example, to propositions that assert or imply that certain physical things exist? Descartes said that we have a 'moral assurance' of the truth of some of the latter propositions but that we lack a 'metaphysical

[1] Some logicians and philosophers have taken an interest in proving that $2 + 2 = 4$ (e.g., Liebniz, *New Essays on the Understanding*, Bk. IV, ch. 7, sec. 10; Frege, *The Foundations of Arithmetic*, sec. 6). They have wished to show that it can be deduced from certain premises, and to determine what premises and rules of inference are required in the deduction. Their interest has not been in the *outcome* of the deduction.

[2] Compare these remarks about the strong sense of 'know' with some of Locke's statements about 'intuitive knowledge': '. . . in this the mind is at no pains of proving or examining . . .' 'This part of knowledge . . . leaves no room for hesitation, doubt, or examination . . .'

'It is on this intuition that depends all the certainty and evidence of all our knowledge; which certainly every one finds to be so great, that he cannot imagine, and therefore not require a greater . . . .' Locke, *Essay*, Bk. IV, ch. 2, sec. 1.

certainty'.[1] Locke said that the perception of the existence of physical things is not 'so certain as our intuitive knowledge, or the deductions of our reason' although 'it is an assurance that deserves the name of knowledge'.[2] Some philosophers have held that when we make judgements of perception such as that there are peonies in the garden, cows in the field, or dishes in the cupboard, we are 'taking for granted' that the peonies, cows, and dishes exist, but not knowing it in the 'strict' sense. Others have held that all empirical propositions, including judgements of perception, are merely hypotheses.[3] The thought behind this exaggerated mode of expression is that any empirical proposition whatever *could* be refuted by future experience—that is, it *could* turn out to be false. Are these philosophers right?

Consider the following propositions:

(i) The sun is about ninety million miles from the earth.
(ii) There is a heart in my body.
(iii) Here is an ink-bottle.

In various circumstances I should be willing to assert of each of these propositions that I know it to be true. Yet they differ strikingly. This I see when, with each, I try to imagine the possibility that it is false.

(i) If in ordinary conversation someone said to me 'The sun is about twenty million miles from the earth, isn't it?' I should reply 'No, it is about ninety million miles from us'. If he said 'I think that you are confusing the sun with Polaris', I should reply, 'I *know* that ninety million miles is roughly the sun's distance from the earth'. I might invite him to verify the figure in an encyclopedia. A third person who overheard our conversation could quite correctly report that I knew the distance to the sun, whereas the other man did not. But this knowledge of mine is little better than hearsay. I have seen that figure mentioned in a few books. I know nothing about the observations and calculations that led astronomers to accept it. If tomorrow a group of eminent astronomers announced that a great error had been made and that the correct figure is twenty million miles, I should not insist that they were wrong. It would surprise me that such an enormous mistake could have been made. But I should no longer be willing to say that I *know* that ninety million is the correct figure.

[1] Descartes, *Discourse on Method*, Part IV.

[2] Locke, *Essay*, Book IV, ch. 11, sec. 3.

[3] e.g., '. . . no proposition, other than a tautology, can possibly be anything more than a probable hypothesis'. A. J. Ayer, *Language, Truth and Logic*, second ed. (New York: Dover Publications, Inc., 1951), p. 38.

Although I should *now* claim that I know the distance to be about ninety million miles, it is easy for me to envisage the possibility that some future investigation will prove this to be false.

(ii) Suppose that after a routine medical examination the excited doctor reports to me that the X-ray photographs show that I have no heart. I should tell him to get a new machine. I should be inclined to say that the fact that I have a heart is one of the few things that I can count on as absolutely certain. I can feel it beat. I know it's there. Furthermore, how could my blood circulate if I didn't have one? Suppose that later on I suffer a chest injury and undergo a surgical operation. Afterwards the astonished surgeons solemnly declare that they searched my chest cavity and found no heart, and that they made incisions and looked about in other likely places but found it not. They are convinced that I am without a heart. They are unable to understand how circulation can occur or what accounts for the thumping in my chest. But they are in agreement and obviously sincere, and they have clear photographs of my interior spaces. What would be my attitude? Would it be to insist that they were all mistaken? I think not. I believe that I should eventually accept their testimony and the evidence of the photographs. I should consider to be false what I now regard as an absolute certainty.

(iii) Suppose that as I write this paper someone in the next room were to call out to me 'I can't find an ink-bottle; is there one in the house?' I should reply 'Here is an ink-bottle'. If he said in a doubtful tone 'Are you sure? I looked there before', I should reply 'Yes, I know there is; come and get it'.

Now could it turn out to be false that there is an ink-bottle directly in front of me on this desk? Many philosophers have thought so. They would say that many things could happen of such a nature that if they did happen it would be proved that I am deceived. I agree that many extraordinary things could happen, in the sense that there is no logical absurdity in the supposition. It could happen that when I next reach for this ink-bottle my hand should seem to pass *through* it and I should not feel the contact of any object. It could happen that in the next moment the ink-bottle will suddenly vanish from sight; or that I should find myself under a tree in the garden with no ink-bottle about; or that one or more persons should enter this room and declare with apparent sincerity that they see no ink-bottle on this desk; or that a photograph taken now of the top of the desk should clearly show all of the objects on it except the ink-bottle. Having admitted that these things *could happen*,[1] am I compelled to admit that if they did happen then it would be proved that there is no ink-bottle here *now*? Not at all! I could say that when my hand seemed to pass through the ink-bottle I should *then* be suffering from hallucination; that if the ink-bottle suddenly vanished it would have miraculously ceased to exist; that the other persons were conspiring to drive me mad, or were themselves victims of remarkable concurrent hallucinations; that the camera possessed some strange flaw or that there was trickery in developing the negative. I admit that in the next moment I could find myself under a tree or in the bathtub. But this is not to admit that it could be revealed in the next moment that I am now dreaming. For what I admit is that I might be instantaneously transported to the garden, but not that in the next moment I might *wake up* in the garden. There is nothing that could happen to me in the next moment that I should call 'waking up'; and therefore nothing that could happen to me in the next moment would be accepted by me now as proof that I now dream.

Not only do I not *have* to admit that those extraordinary occurrences would be evidence that there is no ink-bottle here; the fact is that I *do not* admit it. There is nothing whatever that could happen in the next moment or the next year that would by me be called *evidence* that there is not an ink-bottle here now. No future experience or investigation could prove to me that I am mistaken. Therefore, if I were to say 'I know that there is an ink-bottle here', I should be using 'know' in the strong sense.

It will appear to some that I have adopted an *unreasonable* attitude towards that statement. There is, however, nothing unreasonable about it. It seems so because one thinks that the statement that here is an ink-bottle *must* have the same status as the statements that the sun is ninety million miles away and that I have a heart and that there will be water in the gorge this afternoon. But this is a *prejudice*.

In saying that I should regard nothing as evidence that there is no ink-bottle here now, I am not *predicting* what I should do if various

[1] [My viewpoint is somewhat different here from what it is in 'The Verification Argument'. There I am concerned with bringing out the different ways in which such a remark as 'these things *could* happen' can be taken. I wish to show, furthermore, that from none of the senses in which the remark is *true* does it follow that it is *not certain* that the things in question will *not* happen. Finally, I hold there, that it is perfectly certain that they will not happen. Here I am not disagreeing with any of those points, but I am adding the further point that my admission that, in some sense, the things *could happen*, does not require me to admit that *if* they were to happen, that would be evidence that there is no ink-bottle here now.]

astonishing things happened. If other members of my family entered this room and, while looking at the top of this desk, declared with apparent sincerity that they see no ink-bottle, I might fall into a swoon or become mad. I *might* even come to believe that there is not and has not been an ink-bottle here. I cannot foretell with certainty how I should react. But if it is *not* a prediction, what is the meaning of my assertion that I should regard nothing as evidence that there is no ink-bottle here?

That assertion describes my *present* attitude towards the statement that here is an ink-bottle. It does not prophesy what my attitude *would* be if various things happened. My present attitude towards that statement is radically different from my present attitude towards those other statements (e.g., that I have a heart).[1] I do *now* admit that certain future occurrences would disprove the latter. Whereas no imaginable future occurrence would be considered by me *now* as proving that there is not an ink-bottle here.

These remarks are not meant to be autobiographical. They are meant to throw light on the common concepts of evidence, proof, and disproof. Every one of us upon innumerable occasions of daily life takes this same attitude towards various statements about physical things, e.g., that here is a torn page, that this dish is broken, that the thermometer reads 70, that no rug is on the floor. Furthermore, the concepts of proof, disproof, doubt, and conjecture *require* us to take this attitude. In order for it to be possible that any statements about physical things should *turn out to be false* it is necessary that some statements about physical things *cannot* turn out to be false.

This will be made clear if we ask ourselves the question, When do we *say* that something turned out to be false? When do we use those words? Someone asks you for a dollar. You say 'There is one in this drawer'. You open the drawer and look, but it is perfectly empty. Your statement turned out to be false. This can be said because you *discovered* an empty drawer. It could not be said if it were only probable that the drawer is empty or were still open to question. Would it make sense to say 'I had better make sure that it is empty; perhaps there is a dollar in it after all?' Sometimes; but not always. Not if the drawer lies open before your eyes. That remark is the

[1] [The word 'attitude' is not very satisfactory, but I cannot think of another noun that would do the trick. By 'my attitude' I mean, here, *what I should say and think* if various things were to happen. By 'my *present* attitude' I mean what I should say and think now, when I imagine those things as happening, in contrast with what I should say and think at some future time if those things actually did happen at that time. It is this distinction that shows that my description of 'my present attitude' is not a *prophecy*.]

prelude to a search. What search can there be when the emptiness of the drawer confronts you? In certain circumstances there is nothing that you would call 'making sure' that the drawer is empty; and likewise nothing that you would call 'its turning out to be false' that the drawer is empty. You *made* sure that the drawer is empty. One statement about physical things *turned out to be false* only because you *made sure* of another statement about physical things. The two concepts cannot exist apart. Therefore it is impossible that *every* statement about physical things *could* turn out to be false.

In a certain important respect some a priori statements and some empirical statements possess the same logical character. The statements that $5 \times 5 = 25$ and that here is an ink-bottle, both lie beyond the reach of doubt. On both, my judgement and reasoning *rests*. If you could somehow undermine my confidence in either, you would not teach me *caution*. You would fill my mind with chaos! I could not even make *conjectures* if you took away those fixed points of certainty; just as a man cannot *try* to climb whose body has no support. A conjecture implies an understanding of what certainty would be. If it is not a certainty that $5 \times 5 = 25$ and that here is an ink-bottle, then I do not understand what it is. You cannot make me doubt either of these statements or treat them as hypotheses. You cannot persuade me that future experience could refute them. With both of them it is perfectly unintelligible to me to speak of a 'possibility' that they are false. This is to say that I know both of them to be true, in the strong sense of 'know'. And I am inclined to think that the strong sense of 'know' is what various philosophers have had in mind when they have spoken of 'perfect', 'metaphysical', or 'strict certainty'.[1]

It will be thought that I have confused a statement about my 'sensations', or my 'sense-data', or about the way something *looks* or *appears* to me, with a statement about physical things. It will be thought that the things that I have said about the statement 'Here is an ink-bottle' could be true only if that statement is interpreted to mean something like 'There appears to me to be an ink-bottle here', i.e., interpreted so as not to assert or imply that any physical thing

[1] Descartes, for example, apparently took as his criterion for something's being 'entirely certain' that he could not *imagine* in it the least ground of doubt: '. . . je pensai qu'il fallait . . . que je retasse comme absolument faux tout ce en quoi je pourrais imaginer le moindre doute, afin de voir s'il ne me resterait point après cela quelque chose en ma créance qui fut entièrement indubitable' (*Discourse*, Part IV). And Locke (as previously noted) said of 'intuitive knowledge' that one *cannot imagine* a greater certainty, and that it 'leaves no room for hesitation, doubt, or examination'. *Essay*, Bk. IV, ch. 2, sec. 1.

exists. I wish to make it clear that my statement 'Here is an ink-bottle' is *not* to be interpreted in that way. It would be utterly fantastic for me in my present circumstances to say 'There appears to me to be an ink-bottle here'.

If someone were to call me on the telephone and say that he urgently needed an ink-bottle I should invite him to come here and get this one. If he said that it was extremely urgent that he should obtain one immediately and that he could not afford to waste time going to a place where there might not be one, I should tell him that it is an absolute certainty that there is one here, that nothing could be more certain, that it is something I absolutely guarantee. But if my statement 'There is an ink-bottle here' were a statement about my 'sensations' or 'sense-data', or if it meant that there *appears* to me to be an ink-bottle here or that something here *looks* to me like an ink-bottle, and if that is all that I meant by it—then I should react quite differently to his urgent request. I should say that there is probably an ink-bottle here but that I could not *guarantee* it, and that if he needs one very desperately and at once then he had better look elsewhere. In short, I wish to make it clear that my statement 'Here is an ink-bottle' is strictly about physical things and not about 'sensations', 'sense-data', or 'appearances'.[1]

Let us go back to Prichard's remark that we can determine by reflection whether we know something or merely believe it. Prichard would think that 'knowledge in the weak sense' is mere belief and not knowledge. This is wrong. But if we let ourselves speak this way, we can then see some justification for Prichard's remark. For then he would be asserting, among other things, that we can determine by reflection whether we know something in the strong sense or in the weak sense. This is not literally true; however, there is this truth in it—that reflection can make us realize that we are *using* 'I know it' in the strong (or weak) sense in a particular case. Prichard says that reflection can show us that 'our condition is one of knowing' a certain thing, or instead that 'our condition is one of believing and not of knowing' that thing. I do not understand what could be meant here by 'our condition'. The way I should put it is that reflection on *what we should think* if certain

[1] [The remainder of the essay is newly written. The original conclusion was wrongly stated. The reader is referred to the following exchange between Richard Taylor and myself, in respect to the original paper: Taylor, 'A Note on Knowledge and Belief' *Analysis*, XIII, June 1953; Malcolm, 'On Knowledge and Belief', *Analysis*, XIV, March 1954; Taylor, 'Rejoinder to Mr. Malcolm', ibid.] [Professor Malcolm is here referring to the earlier version of this paper published in *Mind*, Vol. LXI. Ed.]

things were to happen may make us realize that we should (or should not) call those things 'proof' or 'evidence' that what we claim to know is not so. I have tried to show that the distinction between strong and weak knowledge does not run parallel to the distinction between a priori and empirical knowledge but cuts across it, i.e., these two kinds of knowledge may be distinguished *within* a priori knowledge and *within* empirical knowledge.

Reflection can make me realize that I am using 'know' in the strong sense; but can reflection show me that I *know* something in the strong sense (or in the weak)? It is not easy to state the logical facts here. On the one hand, if I make an assertion of the form 'I know that *p*' it does not follow that *p*, whether or not I am using 'know' in the strong sense. If I have said to someone outside my room 'Of course, I know that Freddie is in here', and I am speaking in the strong sense, it does not *follow* that Freddie is where I claim he is. This logical fact would not be altered even if I *realized* that I was using 'know' in the strong sense. My reflection on what I should say if ..., cannot show me that I *know* something. From the fact that I should not call anything 'evidence' that Freddie is not here, it does not follow that he *is* here; therefore, it does not follow that I *know* he is here.

On the other hand, in an actual case of my using 'know' in the strong sense, I cannot envisage a possibility that what I say to be true should turn out to be not true. If I were speaking of *another person's* assertion about something, I *could* think both that he is using 'know' in the strong sense and that nonetheless what he claims he knows to be so might turn out to be not so. But *in my own case* I cannot have this conjunction of thoughts, and this is a logical and not a psychological fact. When *I* say that I know something to be so, using 'know' in the strong sense, it is unintelligible *to me* (although perhaps not to others) to suppose that anything could prove that it is not so and, therefore, that I do not know it.[1]

[1]This is the best summary I can give of what is wrong and right in Prichard's claim that one can determine by reflection whether one knows something or merely believes it. A good part of the ideas in this essay were provoked by conversations with Wittgenstein. A brief and rough account of those talks is to be found in my *Ludwig Wittgenstein: A Memoir* (New York: Oxford University Press, 1958), pp. 87–92. Jaakko Hintikka provides an acute treatment of the topic of 'knowing that one knows', with special reference to Prichard's claim. See his *Knowledge and Belief* (Ithaca: Cornell University Press, 1962), ch. 5.

VI

KNOWING AND NOT KNOWING

A. D. WOOZLEY

MY PURPOSE in the first part of this paper is to call attention to and to correct a mistake which philosophers not uncommonly make when they talk about knowledge. Its latest occurrence known to me is in Professor Malcolm's article 'Knowledge and Belief' in *Mind*, April, 1952.[1] The mistake does not affect his main argument, and I am not here concerned to dispute that. But, as it is a mistake which many of us have frequently made both in print and out of it, it seems worth straightening out on its own account. The tendency to psychologize knowing, even if acts of knowing are not admitted, dies hard, and a part cause of that may be in the continuance of this mistake. It is the mistake of thinking that a man cannot know something unless he is sure of it, of thinking that, as Malcolm puts it (p. 179),[2] 'being confident is a necessary condition for knowing'. In the second part of the paper I want to distinguish it from something else with which it is liable to be confused. Throughout the paper I use 'being sure' as meaning feeling sure, although I recognize that in some expressions and conditions it has different uses.

I

Now prima facie it may seem that to suppose that a man cannot know something unless he is sure of it is not a mistake at all, but obviously true. How could a man know that something was the case if he wasn't sure, or confident, or certain that it was the case? Yet surely

From *Proceedings of the Aristotelian Society*, Vol. 53 (1952–3), pp. 151–72. Reprinted by courtesy of the author and the Editor of the Aristotelian Society.

[1]This statement was true when I wrote it. Since then I have seen a later occurrence in A. C. Ewing's Aristotelian Society paper 'Professor Ryle's Attack on Dualism' (Vol. LII, p. 73).

[2] [p. 70 of the present volume. Ed.]

it is a mistake, concealed by the failure to distinguish a man's knowing that something is the case from his claiming to know that something is the case. Normally he wouldn't make the claim unless he felt sure, and normally, too, our interest in the question whether he knows arises only because he has claimed to know. Yet a man's claim to know, even though he didn't feel sure, even though perhaps he admitted he didn't feel sure, might well be true, although, if he didn't feel sure, he wouldn't have been justified in making it. That is to say, 'I know that *p*, although I'm not sure of it' is not logically self-contradictory, any more than 'I think that it is raining, although it isn't' is logically self-contradictory. But 'I know that *p*, although I'm not sure of it' would have to be self-contradictory, if being sure is a necessary condition of knowing.

'I think that it is raining, although it isn't' could perfectly well be true, namely if uttered by a speaker at a time when, although it was in fact not raining, he thought that it was raining. What is wrong with his statement is not that it is logically self-contradictory, or that it cannot be true, but that it is epistemologically absurd, it cannot be a statement which a man would ever be justified in making; for any reasons that he could have to support the opinion that it was raining would be reasons against his making the statement that it wasn't raining.[1] Therefore, although the whole statement might be truly made, it could never be justifiably made. (I've already spoken, and shall again, of a claim to know being true. If it seems objectionable to talk of claims being true (or false), I should be understood to be using the phrase 'claim to know being true' as meaning the same as the phrase 'statement that one knows being true'.)

I suggest that somewhat similar considerations apply to 'I know that *p*, although I'm not sure of it'. What is wrong with that statement too is not that it couldn't be true, but that I couldn't be justified in making it. (I am saying, not that there are *no* logical differences between my two examples, but that in this respect they are similar.) The question whether I know that something is the case is the same as the question whether I can *truly* claim to know that it is the case (i.e., whether, if I make the claim, it is true); but it is not the same as the question whether I can *justifiably* claim to know that it is the case. The question whether I can truly claim to know that it is the case

[1]Unfortunately Max Black's article 'Saying and Disbelieving' (*Analysis*, Vol. 13, No. 2) appeared too shortly before the printing of this paper for me to discuss his arguments, which would be arguments against a position of the sort that I am suggesting.

the case is the question whether I know that it is the case; the question whether I can justifiably claim to know that it is the case is the question whether my reasons for saying that I know that it is the case are good reasons. Being sure that it is the case is a necessary condition of my claim's being justifiable; but that does not entail that it is a necessary condition of the claim's being true; and I am prepared to deny that it is a necessary condition of that.

This can be brought out by considering the case of different speakers. Suppose the question to be whether A knows that *p*. Then, if A feels uncertain of *p*, it would be unreasonable, epistemologically absurd, for him to say that he knew that *p*. But B might be able both truly and justifiably to say that A knew that *p*—truly, because A does know that *p*, justifiably, because he can do what A at present cannot do, viz., show that A does know that *p*. Examples of this are very commonly provided in the case of 'knowing how': A claiming that he doesn't know how to do something, and B replying that he (A) knows perfectly well how to do it, or that he (A) really does know how to do it, although he (A) thinks he doesn't. B can often follow up this reply by *showing* A that he does know. The fact that A felt unsure, or didn't think he knew was a good reason for *his* not claiming to know; but it would not follow from that that he didn't know; nor would that necessarily be a good reason for B's not claiming that A knew. Similarly for cases of 'knowing that'. Just as sometimes I can show A that his statement 'I know that *p*' is false, so sometimes I can show A that his statement 'I don't know that *p*' is false. I shall return shortly to the question of knowing that *p* while being unsure of it.

Here I should interject that what I have said and what I am going to say about knowing should not be taken to apply to all kinds of knowing. It may so apply, but I'm not concerned here to argue that it does. The cases which I am not considering are those which may here be called direct knowledge, e.g., knowing that something happened because one saw it happen. My concern is with the other kind, where the knowing could be represented as an inference (not necessarily that it was actually reached inferentially). This is the kind of case where 'Do you know?' is contrasted with 'Do you believe?' and not the kind of case where 'Do you know?' is contrasted with 'Are you unaware?', and where equivalent questions are 'Have you seen?', 'Have you heard?', 'Have you been told?', etc. Nor am I concerned with the case, if it is a different case—if indeed it is a case at all—of knowing that I have a pain because I feel it.

No doubt the kind of knowing with which I am concerned and the kind of knowing with which I am not concerned shade off into each other, but that is not to say that they are not distinguishable.

It is sometimes said that a statement of the form 'A knows that *p*' varies in meaning according as the speaker is A or somebody else, i.e., that 'know' operates differently in 'I know that *p*' (said by A) from the way it operates in 'He knows that *p*' (said of A by somebody else); and it may seem that this is the direction in which I have been arguing. But it isn't, for I wish to deny that the meaning of the statement varies with the speaker, or that 'know' operates one way autobiographically, another way biographically. I see no reason for denying that it operates the same way in both cases. So also with 'A doesn't know that *p*'. A difference may well lie in the context: A may have quite different reasons for making the statement about himself from those that B has from making the statement about him; and what A wants to *do* by his statement (as opposed to what he *says* by it) may well be different from what B wants to do by his statement. Consequently when A asserts 'I don't know that *p*' and B denies 'A doesn't know that *p*' (i) B is denying exactly what A is asserting, (ii) one or other of them is right, (iii) it can as well be B that is right as be A that is right; and sometimes it is B that is right, (iv) but, although what A says is false (we'll suppose), he may be justified in saying it. If he didn't feel sure of *p*, he had good reason for saying that he didn't know *p*. But that doesn't necessarily give us good reason for saying that he didn't know that *p*. Once more, being sure or being confident cannot be a necessary condition for knowing.

The test of whether I know is what I can do, where what I can do may include answering questions. If I can do the right things and give the right answers, and if I can also show that they are the right things to do and the right answers to give, am I to be denied knowledge, just because I go through the performance in a way that shows that I am not confident that it is the right performance or that I am showing that it is? If I am to be denied it, and if being sure is necessary to knowing, then many candidates at *viva voce* examinations have been credited with knowledge which they haven't got.

But in fact if, as sometimes happens, one suspects fellow examiners of crediting a candidate with knowledge which he hasn't got, it is for a different reason, viz., because one suspects that although the candidate has given the right answers he couldn't show that they were right: and the examiners have been hoodwinked by his apparent (maybe real, too) confidence into thinking he does know. They have been hoodwinked because often enough when a man does know he is confident, and because consequently one is liable to treat confidence as a better sign of knowledge than it is. Again, often enough when a man does not know he lacks confidence, and consequently one is liable to treat lack of confidence as a better sign of ignorance than it is. In short, not only is confidence not a sufficient condition of knowing (which nobody would seriously maintain), but also it is not a necessary condition of knowing either (which plenty of philosophers have maintained). The mistake of supposing that it is a necessary condition of knowing is somewhat similar, although pushed one stage further back, to the not uncommon mistake of supposing that a man cannot validly infer q from p unless he knows that p implies q; that is to confuse doing a valid inference with being able to meet successfully a challenge to its validity; to confuse using a rule with being able to defend the rule against attack.

This, in a sense, is the end of my story. But it is not the end of my paper, for I want to go on to consider objections which have been made to it, to distinguish it from something else which has been confused with it, and to ask whether any philosophical morals are to be drawn at the end.

It has been objected that what I am maintaining, viz., that being sure or confident is not necessary to knowing, may be tenable in the case of knowing how, but is not tenable in the case of knowing that, and perhaps that this is one of the distinguishing marks between knowing how and knowing that. That it is sense, for instance, to say to a man 'You think you don't know how to solve that problem (work out that equation; discover the firing order of the cylinders in your car, etc.), but you do really'; but that it is not sense to say to a man 'You think you don't know that today is Thursday; Hitler is dead; the Keynes who wrote the *Treatise on Probability* was the same man as the Keynes who wrote *The Economic Consequences of the Peace*; etc., but you do really'.

Now the first thing that needs to be said in this connexion is that the knowing how—knowing that antithesis is nothing like as simple as we are liable to make it. For 'knowing how' is riddled with ambiguities. Some of them, perhaps, don't matter here (I mention two, in order to say that they are *not* what I'm talking about), e.g.:

1. (*a*) Knowing how = (roughly) being able as a result of having learned, *as opposed to*

(*b*) Knowing how = (roughly) knowing what is required to be done, but being unable, through some defect or deficiency, to do it. E.g., knowing how, as an actor, to speak a certain line, but being unable through stage fright to do it; knowing how to thread a needle, but being unable through poor eyesight or an unsteady hand to do it.

2. (*a*) Knowing how in sense 1 (*a*) above, *as opposed to*

(*b*) Knowing how in the sense not merely of being able, but of being able to do well, with great skill. E.g., 'There's a man who knows how to . . . bowl to his field, drive a car, play chess, etc.' This use is commonly qualified emphatically. 'If you want to find a man who really knows how to tune your car, go to Jones.' 'He's a man who does know how to get things done.'

But there is a third 'knowing-how' ambiguity which does matter here.

3. (*a*) 'Knowing how' is commonly followed by what, for classification's sake, I may be allowed to call simple verbs of action where what I know how to do is what, barring accidents, I straightway do, if I try to do it. E.g., knowing how to swim, ride a bicycle, use chopsticks, etc.

(*b*) What I mean by calling these simple verbs of action may be made clearer by turning to the other use of 'knowing how' to be contrasted with them, the use according to which what I know how to do is to achieve a certain result. The clearest cases here will be those where the process of getting to the result is a comparatively long one. Success in case (*a*) consists in doing the thing, and maybe in keeping on doing the thing; success in case (*b*) consists in completing the thing, i.e., in getting through the necessary stages of the process in such a way that the end is achieved. (*a*) would be exemplified by knowing how to dribble the ball, (*b*) by knowing how to score a goal, or even knowing how to get the ball into the opponent's net. Trying to dribble a ball stands in a different relation to dribbling it, from the relation between trying to score a goal and scoring it.

Perhaps a clearer example of this second use of 'knowing how' would be provided by some supposedly more intellectual activity than playing football. E.g., knowing how to score a grand slam at bridge, which involves at the least having some views about or making some judgements about the effects of playing the cards in a certain order, about the likely distribution of the five clubs which one's opponents hold between them, about the location of the one king which neither oneself nor dummy holds, etc. We would, I think, hesitate to say of a man that he knew how to make a grand slam, in circumstances in which it was admittedly makeable, if he could give no reasonable account of the way in which he went about making it, or of the considerations which weighed with him in the course of the playing of the hand. Even if he could give such an account, we should still hesitate to say he knew how, if his account showed that he had been banking on improbable contingencies, which nevertheless came off. Even if he persistently brought off a high proportion of his slam bids in such circumstances, we should, I think, prefer to say he was lucky at cards, or that he had an uncanny knack of reaching his bids, than to say he knew how.

The point of this example, and of teasing out this 'know-how' ambiguity is this: that knowing how to achieve a certain result by going through a certain preliminary process designed to achieve that result seems to involve some knowing that, or at least some reasonably believing that; whereas on the other hand, knowing how to perform actions of the swimming, riding a bicycle, eating with chopsticks kind, does not seem to involve any knowing or believing that about intermediary steps likely to bring about the desired results, for the simple reason that there aren't any intermediary steps. Swimming involves the contraction and expansion of all kinds of muscles, but I don't try to contract and expand muscles, the contraction and expansion of which would result in my swimming. I can swim, but I do it by trying to swim, not by trying to contract and expand my muscles, nor by formulating probability-beliefs about which muscles to contract and expand.

Consequently, if there is a knowing how which does involve a knowing that, or at the least a reasonably believing that, and another knowing how which doesn't involve that—which I hope I have succeeded in showing—then the fact that being sure or confident is not essential to the latter, simpler kind of knowing how does not entail that it is not essential to the former. To make up our minds whether or not it is essential to the former we must look more at knowing that. This is what I was getting at in saying earlier that the knowing how-knowing that antithesis was not as simple as we are inclined to make it.

So far, then, it seems that at any rate in some cases of knowing how, although not yet certainly in all, a man can know how without being sure how; he can think he doesn't know how and yet know how; and he can think he knows how. If now for 'know how' we substitute 'know that' are the new statements true?

(1) Can a man know that without being sure that?
(2) Can he think he doesn't know that, and yet know that?
(3) Can he think he knows that?

About knowing that, without being sure that, I have not much more to say. For me to know that *p*, it must be the case that *p* is true, that I have sufficient reasons for asserting *p*, and that if I do assert *p*, I assert it for these reasons. It need not be the case that I should know that they are sufficient reasons; for example, I might think that my reasons only made *p* probable, whereas in fact (as you might be able to show me) they were conclusive reasons. The instances that spring to mind are all of a more or less irrational kind; but that is hardly surprising, for to say of a man that he knows that *p*, although he is not sure of it is to criticize him for being somehow irrational, for not being sure of something of which he ought to be sure. The man who knows that he has just got something that he has terribly wanted such as promotion or a particular appointment, not only says that he cannot really believe it, but may really not be able to believe it—until he is actually sitting at the new desk or wearing the new badges with nobody stopping him. Another type of case is that where it is vitally important not to be wrong: one knows that he has locked the door of the safe, but feels obliged to go back to make sure. Cases such as these are quite different from another, with which they might be confused, and which, if the distinction were not drawn, might be adduced against me. This is the case of the man, recently bereaved of an old friend or close relative, saying that he cannot really believe that the friend or relative is dead. In such a case as this one does believe that the friend is dead, has no doubt about that, but has difficulty in yet adjusting one's conduct and expectations to the belief; it is not a case of knowing but not being sure, for it is not a case of not being sure. The difference between it and the others which are cases of that is that in them one's hesitation, from whatever caution or irrational source it may spring, is in admitting as sufficient evidence what clearly is sufficient evidence, and what in another context in which one was less personally involved, one would not hesitate to admit as sufficient evidence.

I admit that there does seem something queer about a man thinking he doesn't know that something is the case, but nevertheless knowing that something is the case; or even about his thinking that he knows that something is the case. But even if they turn out too queer to pass, they don't carry down with them that a man can't know that without being sure that. For thinking that I know that *p* (if that turns out to be permissible) would be a way of not being sure that I know that *p*, and does not look to be the same as knowing that *p* but not being sure that *p*; not being sure that I know that *p* is not being sure that *q*, where *q* is the proposition that I know that *p*, and whereas not being sure that *p* does entail not being sure that *q*, not being sure that *q* does not entail not being sure that *p*. Another way of bringing out the difference between on the one hand knowing that but not being sure that and on the other hand thinking that one does not know that would be to point out that even if Malcolm is right, as I have tried to argue that he is not, in holding a view a corollary of which is that 'You know that *p*, although you're not sure that *p*' is self-contradictory, the view would not have as a corollary that 'You think you don't know that *p*, but you do' is self-contradictory. For in the sense of 'know' which is under discussion a man might quite well think that he didn't know that *p*, even though he was sure that *p*, e.g., that his horse would win the 2.30. In any case where a man was sure that *p* the conjunctive assertion that he knew that *p* although he was not sure that *p* would be false and necessarily false; in the same case the conjunctive assertion that he thought that he did not know that *p* but he did know that *p* might be false, but it would not be necessarily false, and, as I shall try to show, it might be true.

One reason for the queerness of 'thinks he knows that' or 'thinks he doesn't know that' is something less to do with knowing and not knowing than with a habit of English usage, or rather with two habits.

(1) If we look for differences between 'know', according as it is followed by 'that' on the one hand, or by any of the interrogatives (not merely 'how') on the other, one very obvious one stands out. It is a feature of 'know' followed by 'how', 'what', 'where', 'when', 'whether', etc., that it raises a question, perhaps if the sentence is in the indicative indicates that it is answerable, but does not answer it. But in the case of 'knowing that' it is just the other way round. The question is answered, without, as it were, having been asked. E.g., if I say 'Jones knows what time the train goes . . . which platform it goes from . . . whether it has a restaurant car . . . etc.', I raise a number of questions, don't answer any of them, but assert that Jones can give the answer. But if I say 'Jones knows that the train goes at 2.10 . . . leaves from the front of No. 1 . . . etc.', I'm giving the answer without asking for questions.

For it to be true that Jones knows what time the train goes, it must at least be the case that Jones can give the right answer, if he wants, to the question what time the train goes. And in telling you that he knows what time it goes, I'm not doing more for you than assuring you that in this matter at least you can trust Jones.

But if I say that 'Jones knows that the train goes at 2.10' I am doing more for you, something I'm not doing in the first case—I'm telling you what time the train goes. In all reports of the form 'X knows that . . . ' the speaker endorses what follows the 'that'. In reporting that Jones knows that the train goes at 2.10 I'm committing myself not merely to something definite about Jones but also to something definite about the train. In the other case, in reporting that he knows what time it goes, I'm committing myself to something definite about Jones, but to nothing definite about the train—except that it goes at whatever time Jones will say it goes, if you ask him and if he wants to give you the right answer.

Even in the interrogative form 'know that' almost always commits the speaker to what follows, whereas 'know what, where, why, . . . etc.' don't even commit him to being able to answer the question if asked. 'Do you know that . . . it's raining? . . . today's my birthday? . . . John and Mary are engaged? . . . jet engines run on kerosene?, etc.', all tell you, whether or not you want or need to be told, that what follows the 'that' is the case. That is, even in the case where I'm asking you whether you know I'm telling you what it is that you must know for it to be true that you do know. The only case where the speaker is not committed to what follows the 'that' is the one where the 'know' is heavily emphasized. 'Do you *know* that the Minister drinks like a fish?' By emphasizing the 'know' in that way, I'm not at all committing myself to the view that the Minister drinks like a fish. I may hold the view that he does, or that he doesn't, or I may have no view about it at all. I may not even much be interested in the question of his drinking, but only in the question of the responsibility or irresponsibility of your statement that he does.

(2) The second linguistic habit I want to refer to is one connected with prefixing 'he knows' with 'he thinks'. 'He thinks he knows' seems to be used *either* in the case where the speaker wishes to remain neutral, and not commit himself to saying that the man does know, or that he doesn't, *or* in the case where the speaker wishes to discredit the claim. I.e., *either* 'He thinks he knows, but I can't say whether he does or not' *or* 'He thinks he knows, but he certainly doesn't'. There doesn't seem to be a use for the third case 'He thinks he knows, and he certainly does'. The point about 'He thinks he knows' is that it is not simply reproducing in the third person a statement which the agent in question has made or would make in the first person, 'I think I know'. 'He thinks he knows' is the way of commenting, or of

beginning to comment on, the agent's claim to know, not his claim to think he knows. There's no point in reporting him as thinking he knows, unless either you're not prepared to endorse his claim (nor to deny it), or you are prepared to deny it. If you're prepared to endorse it, you say that he knows.

If you now consider these two habits together (1) The contrast between 'knows what, when, whether . . . etc.' and 'knows that . . . ' and (2) The function of 'he thinks he knows . . . ', you'll see why 'he thinks he knows that . . . ' is queer. From (1) we get that what follows 'knows that . . . ' is the case, i.e., is endorsed by the speaker. From (2) we get that what follows 'he thinks he knows . . . ' is not endorsed by the speaker. So while we are prepared to say 'He thinks he knows the answer, but he doesn't' or 'He thinks he knows what time the train goes, but he doesn't', we are not so prepared to say 'He thinks he knows that the train goes at 2.10, but he doesn't'.

But that we don't, or are reluctant to, say that a man thinks that he knows that something is the case, but he doesn't, doesn't entail that a man never does or cannot think that he knows that something is the case (whether or not he doesn't). And the dangers of jumping between the formal and material modes of speech are well illustrated here. Even if I am right in my argument that we find something queer about 'He thinks he knows that . . .', that phrase doesn't misdescribe or fail to describe the situation in which a man might say 'I think I know that . . . '. It would misdescribe or fail to describe the situation in which a man might say 'I know that . . .'. We still have on our hands the question whether a man might say 'I think I know that . . . '.

There is undeniably something odd about 'I think I know that . . .', whereas there's nothing at all odd about 'I think I know . . . ' with any of the interrogatives. 'I think I know where he lives . . . why he left in a hurry . . . which way he went . . . etc.' but not 'I think I know that my redeemer liveth'. Is there then no such thing as thinking that one knows that, where the phrase, if it reports anything, reports the claim to think one knows that, not the claim to know that? One is naturally tempted to reply that there isn't, and to point out that if there were, one wouldn't find the form 'I think I know that . . . ' as odd as one does. Nevertheless it seems to be clear that there is such a thing as thinking that I know that, and that the oddity of the phrase can be accounted for by the rarity of the occasions on which it would be correct to use it.

One reason I've met for saying that it doesn't make sense to say 'I think I know that . . . ' is that its logical consequences are absurd. For, to take an example, 'I think I know the train goes at 2.10' seems to entail 'I think that the train goes at 2.10'; and if I think that the train goes at 2.10, I oughtn't to say I know, or even I think I know, that it goes at 2.10.

Now, there seem to be at least two doubtful points about that argument.

(*a*) Is it at all clear that 'I think I know that . . . ' does entail 'I think that . . . '? If one tries doubting the entailment, it is hard to see how to remove the doubt. Thinking that one knows that isn't a conjunctive whole, such that if the whole is the case a part is the case. The view that thinking one knows that entails thinking that seems to confuse thinking that one knows that with knowing that but not being sure that. The latter does seem to entail thinking that; but I'm inclined to think that a man who said he thought he knew that would not agree that he thought that; he would simply insist that he thought he knew that. Just what he would mean by it remains still to be elucidated.

(*b*) The other doubtful point about the argument comes in the final stage, where it is asserted that if I think that the train goes at 2.10, I oughtn't to say I know, or even that I think I know that it goes at 2.10. What sort of 'ought' is that? If what is being asserted is that if I say I think the train goes at 2.10, I'm not justified in, or I haven't sufficient reason for, saying that I know that, or that I think I know that, the train goes at 2.10, I have no objection. But this wouldn't entail that my statement that I know that, or that I thought I knew that, was false. It might still be true. This part of the argument in fact confuses again the distinction between justifiably claiming to know (or to think I know) with truly claiming to know (or to think I know) which I referred to at the beginning of the paper, and which I needn't discuss again now.

So what I'm saying here is:

(*a*) I doubt that 'I think I know that' does entail 'I think that'.

(*b*) Even if it does, I doubt if it matters. A somewhat analogous case, where it clearly doesn't matter, would be that of 'I think I know . . . ' followed by one of the interrogatives. Suppose I think I know what time the train goes, suppose that the time I mention is 2.10, and suppose that 2.10 is in fact the time at which the train goes. Here surely is a case where (i) you should say I did know what time the train went, but (ii) I should have to say not that I knew that it went at 2.10, but that I thought it went at 2.10. So 'I think I know that . . .' entails 'I think that . . .', and we don't suggest that the fact that it entails that itself entails that it isn't sense to say 'I think I know what . . .'

Now, I don't want to press this analogy too far, because it won't go very far. That it doesn't serves to illuminate a quite important difference between thinking that one knows what (whether, why, when, etc.) and thinking that one knows that, and it throws some light on the latter and on the conditions in which it would be correct to say that I think I know that.

There is quite a striking and, I think, here relevant difference between the way in which 'knowing what' (or 'know' with any of the other interrogatives) operates and the way in which 'know that' operates. In the case of 'know' with an interrogative, we allow that a man knows, or we accept his claim to know, if he can give the right answer, solve the problem, or do the trick. But in the case of knowing that, that is not enough. Suppose, for example, when I go to start my car one morning, nothing will induce it to start. I go through all the usual drill, turn the engine on, choke it, press the starter button until the battery is almost dead, flood the carburettor, and swing the starter handle until I'm exhausted—all without getting a kick out of the engine. Suppose you, knowing more about these things than I do, having first tested the spark and the petrol supply and found both satisfactory, say 'I know what's wrong—your plugs are (must be) wet'. We take out the plugs, and find they're soaking wet. I ask you whether you know what to do to put things right. You say Yes, the best thing to do is to get a rag, soak it in petrol, put the plugs on it, set fire to the rag, and after a minute or so put out the fire, and replace the plugs in the engine. We do just that, and the car starts at the first push on the button. Surely we should say that you did know what was wrong, and that you did know what to do about it. Similarly with 'Do you know what the time is, please?', or in its more quaintly idiomatic form 'Do you know what the right time is, please?', 'Do you know which is Mrs. Jones's house?'. 'Do you know . . . what, etc.?', in fact, is often virtually interchangeable with 'Can you tell me . . . what etc?' The proof of the pudding is in the eating. If you make the thing work, or give the right answer, we would allow that you did know. Further, and this is important, if one wants to be critical of a man's claim to know what and to suggest that his success in making the thing work, or in giving the right answer was a fluke or a lucky guess, one asks a know *that* question. 'Did you know that that was what was wrong with the engine? . . . that that was what you had to do to the plugs to get the car to start?'

For, in the case of knowing that, giving the right answer isn't enough. For us to allow that you know that, you must be able to convince us that you had shown or could show (to anyone informed and intelligent enough to follow) that it was or must be the right answer. You knew that it must be that the plugs were wet because you had eliminated, by testing the spark and the petrol flow, the other things that could prevent the engine from firing.

In short, the claim to know what (when, whether . . . etc.) is a more limited claim than the claim to know that; and this, in turn, affects the issue when we turn back from 'I know' to 'I think I know'.

(*a*) 'I think I know what (when, where, etc.) . . .' is the appropriate thing to say when I think I can give the right answer. It is, in fact, a milder, more cautious claim than 'I know what . . .'. It is a way of admitting that the answer I'm prepared to put forward *may* not be right, whereas 'I know what . . .' doesn't admit that at all, but insists that my answer, if I give it, *is* right.

(*b*) On the other hand, as I've suggested earlier, 'I think I know that . . .' is not the appropriate thing to say when I think (as opposed to know) that what follows the 'that' is right. 'I think I know that . . .' might be true in such a situation, but it couldn't be a justifiable claim to make, for any reasons I had *for* saying that I thought (as opposed to know) that what followed the 'that' was right would be reasons *against* making any claim, even a mild one, to know.

It rather seems to me that 'I think I know that . . .' is the appropriate thing to say, when what is in question is not so much what follows the 'that' (it may not even be in question at all) but my claim to know it. In other words, a man claims to think he knows that, not when he thinks (as opposed to knows) the answer is right, but when he thinks (as opposed to knows) that he can show it to be right, that his reasons for saying it to be right *are* good and sufficient reasons for saying it to be right.

'I think I know that . . .' in fact = 'I think I can truly say I know that . . .', i.e., if I say I know that what I say will be true.

Compare once more 'Do you know that the Minister drinks like a fish?', which among other things tells you that he does, and 'Do you *know* that the Minister drinks like a fish?', which doesn't tell you that he does, which may not suggest any disbelief that he does, but which does ask you whether you *know* that he does. And to that question the answer might in certain circumstances be 'Yes, I think I do know . . .'. In the Burgess and Maclean case, while few of us have any doubt in which direction in general they went, few of us too would say we knew that they had gone behind the Iron Curtain. But the Foreign Office man, or the *Daily Express* man, put on to investigate the case, might reach a point in his investigation when, if asked 'Do you know that they went behind the Iron Curtain?', he would reply 'Yes, I think I do know that they did'. Mr. Trevor Roper, or any of the others put on to clean up Hitler's fate at the end of the war, might well, at a certain stage in the research, have said that at last he thought he knew that Hitler was dead—i.e., at last he thought he could truly say that he knew that Hitler was dead, at last he thought his reasons for saying Hitler was dead were sufficient.

Here, again, is a reason for not confusing knowing that but not being sure that with thinking that one knows that. While, as I argued at the beginning, knowing that but not being sure that is a perfectly possible state to be in, it cannot ever be sensible for a man to say he is in it, although it may be sensible for others to say he is in it. On the other hand thinking that one knows that is a perfectly possible state to be in, and it can be sensible for a man to say he is in it—while, if others say he is in it, they mean something quite different.

And the reason for the rarity of the phrase 'think I know that' is surely the rarity of the situation calling for it:

(*a*) Far more often than not, whenever a man makes a claim (strong or mild) that something is the case, we're more interested in what follows the 'that' than in what precedes it. One doesn't feel outraged if, when one has said 'I think that it is raining', somebody goes to the window and replies 'No, it isn't', or even 'No, you're wrong, it isn't'. And, if a man says that he knows that something is the case, one far more often takes him up when one is inclined to question whether it is the case than when one is inclined to question whether he *knows* that it is so. No doubt the second type of question occurs more often in the courts, but my restricted knowledge of the law leads me to suspect that it is a little simple-minded over the use of words such as 'know'; and that if a man were to say in court that he thought he knew that something was the case, he would either be told that that showed that he didn't know (which, if I am right, would be untrue), or be told to answer unequivocally—either he did know or he didn't (which would surely be true but, if I am right, irrelevant).

To ask the question 'How did he know that . . . ?' or 'How could he have known that . . . ?' (without any special emphasis on the 'know'), implies acceptance of what follows the 'that', and asks a question only about the person. One may be allowing that he did know, and be enquiring how he came to know or to find out; or one may be querying whether he did know, and be asking to be shown that he did (if he did). In the former case the contrast is between various possible ways of knowing, or methods of finding out; in the latter case the contrast is not (yet, at any rate) between them, for he may not have known at all, but between his knowing at all and his having made a lucky guess. Where the 'know' is emphasized and the question is 'How did he *know* that . . . ?' one is not committing oneself to the truth of what follows the 'that'. It may indeed be this that one is primarily interested in querying, but more usually one would be querying not this (N.B.—not to be querying this is not the same as to be accepting it) but whether, even if this was true, he knew it rather than wrongly thought he knew it.

(*b*) When one does question not whether something is the case (or, at any rate, not primarily whether it is the case), but whether the man *knows* that it is the case, it is naturally much more common to get the answer 'Yes' or 'Yes I do', than the more sophisticated answer 'Yes, I think I do'. It is a more sophisticated answer, because it isn't a straightforward reply to the question 'Do you know?', but rather a second-order reply that you thought the first-order reply 'Yes' would be (or is) true, that your reasons for saying that something is the case are sufficient.

In fact, unless the question 'Do you know?' is asked, one seldom uses the phrase 'I know that . . .', except by way of emphasis, to stress that what follows is quite certainly true. And 'I *think* I know that . . .' gives a poor sort of emphasis, so one doesn't use it unless challenged; and when challenged, one isn't all that often cautious enough to stand back a pace and say that he thinks that it is true (or that he is entitled) to say that he knows; but one is sometimes.

All that I have left are the summarizing and the moralizing, both of which can be mercifully brief. But I should add that I'm not clear that my account of thinking one knows that, as given in these last few pages, is correct. I have, in my own mind, wavered between two versions of 'I think I know that' as = (1) 'I think my reasons for saying that are sufficient', or (2) 'I think my reasons for saying I know that justify saying I know that'.

(1) is the version I have used. I am not sure that (2) isn't correct.

Summary

(1) Knowing, but not being sure—both with the interrogatives and with 'that'—is perfectly possible, and actual. But the phrase, used autobiographically, is absurd, in the same sort of way as 'I think it's raining, but it isn't' is absurd—which doesn't prevent its being true.

(2) Thinking that one knows

(*a*) differs from (1) in the ways I have outlined,

(*b*) is possible both with the interrogatives and with 'that'. In the case of the interrogatives, the suggestion is that the answer one is prepared to give *may* not be the right one. In the case of 'that', the suggestion is not that the answer may not be the right one, but that it may not be true that one knows it (one's reasons for giving it may not be sufficient). (*Or* that one may not be *justified* in saying that one knows it.)

(3) 'He thinks he knows' and 'I think I know' differ not merely in person, but also in the kind of claim that is made or queried.

Morals

(1) We shouldn't oversimplify the contrast between knowing how and knowing that (*a*) because of the different kinds of knowing how—the various ambiguities of the phrase 'know how', (*b*) because at least one kind of knowing how, the knowing how to produce a certain result by a certain method, involves a knowing that.

(2) Knowing isn't the one really good, 100 per cent., unassailable self-certifying thing we do, that many philosophers, as various as Plato, Descartes, and Prichard, would have us believe (*a*) because it isn't something we do, it's something we get to by what we do; (*b*) because although to say that a man knows is to make a 100 per cent. claim, it may not be a claim which he is in a position to make for himself; (*c*) because knowing isn't self-certifying, as you can know but not know that you know, just as much as you can wrongly think you know and not know that you're wrongly thinking it. (Descartes had at least some inkling of this in the difficulties which he admitted over his notion of clear and distinct perception.) (*d*) Of all the mental words, such that when you use them you're supposedly talking about a man's activities, or condition, etc., 'knowledge' is traditionally the favourite, but has a poor enough claim to be so. In a way, it is the least personal of them all. For when we say that a man knows something, we are not merely reporting something about him, as we are when we say that he believes something, we are also (although this

isn't all that we are also doing) making a comment about him, that his answers are the right answers—or, if he hasn't yet given them, that if he gives them, and if he wants them to be the right answers, they will be the right answers. Although Professor Ryle was wrong in contrasting belief and knowledge as tendency and capacity (wrong because knowledge is as much (or as little) a tendency as belief), yet there was a point in his contrast—that we do not allow that a man knows unless his answers are right. While it is nowadays widely held that if we classify 'knowing' and 'believing' as psychological verbs, yet we should distinguish them from other occurrent psychological verbs such as 'wonder', 'reflect', 'consider', etc., it is not yet sufficiently admitted how little 'know' is a psychological verb at all. (*e*) Maybe we ought to say 'I think I know that . . .' more often than we do. Perhaps we avoid the more modest claim than that 'I know that . . .' because it seems to be an admission that we don't know; but, as I've tried to argue, it doesn't admit that.

In short, perhaps, the notion of knowledge stands in need of some deflation. For it is a much more complicated and diverse business than philosophers are liable to allow; and consequently it is both more difficult and more dangerous to generalize about it in the simple way we do than we commonly recognize.

VII

ON CLAIMING TO KNOW

ALAN R. WHITE

PROFESSOR A. D. Woozley has made what I believe to be an important distinction between 'claiming to know' and 'knowing',[1] from which it follows that

> the question whether I can truly claim to know that it is the case is the question whether I know that it is the case; the question whether I can justifiably claim to know that it is the case is the question whether my reasons for saying that I know that it is the case are good reasons. Being sure that it is the case is a necessary condition of my claim's being justifiable; but that does not entail that it is a necessary condition of the claim's being true; and I am prepared to deny that it is a necessary condition of that.

I wish to show that there are several important conclusions to be drawn from this distinction other than those which Woozley has drawn and that most of these are intimately linked with one conclusion which he expressly and, as I shall argue, wrongly repudiates. In short, I wish to suggest certain addenda and corrigenda to his valuable paper.

I would take the passage just quoted to assert—though Woozley does not put it like this—that the criteria for judging the making of a claim, that is, whether the claim is reasonable or unreasonable, are those of confidence and good evidence, while the criterion for judging the claim itself, that is, whether the claim is valid or not, is that of truth. These three criteria are, of course, those which are usually taken together as relevant to the assessment of the validity of a claim. It seems to me the great merit of Woozley's distinction is

From *Philosophical Review*, Vol. 66 (1957), pp. 180–92. Reprinted by permission of the author and the *Philosophical Review*.

[1] 'Knowing and Not Knowing', *Proc. Aristotelian Society*, LIII (1953), esp. pp. 151–156. [pp. 82–86 of this volume. Ed.]

that it supports our natural inclination to hold, against the usual view, that the confidence of the man who says he knows so-and-so is irrelevant to judging whether he does or not; and that it supports also our inclination to suppose that a man knows something even when, it being the sort of thing for which there are reasons, he cannot give any of them. There are qualifications to be made to this, some given by Woozley and others which I shall add later.

We have then to distinguish four things, namely, the making of a claim, the claim itself, the judgement on the former, and the judgement on the latter. Correspondingly, and this is the point I want chiefly to make in opposition to Woozley, there are important logical differences in the different forms of the verb 'to know' which are used to express three of these. We make a claim by saying, 'I (we) know' and perhaps report another's making a claim by, 'He (you) says he (you) knows'; we judge the making of a claim, that is, the reasonableness of a claim, by saying, 'He (you) would be correct (justified) in saying he (you) knows'; we judge the claim itself, that is, the validity of the claim, by saying either what we said in judging its reasonableness or, more commonly, 'He (you) knows'. By bringing out the logical differences of these forms, especially the differences between 'I know' and 'He knows' and the differences hidden in the one expression 'He (you) would be correct (justified) in saying that he (you) knows', I hope to show that Woozley is wrong in denying 'that "know" operates differently in "I know that *p*" (said by *A*) from the way that it operates in "He knows that *p*" (said of *A* by somebody else)'. 'I know' is used to make a claim; 'He knows' or 'You know' to endorse or allow, to judge favourably, a claim. Similarly, 'I don't know' refuses to make a claim, while 'He doesn't know' rejects a claim. The role of claimant is quite different from that of judge; both use the same language for quite different purposes.

A lack of clarity about the use of 'I know' to make claims leads to several mistakes in the relation of 'feeling sure' to 'knowing'. I shall draw attention to two which are plausible and which, occurring after Woozley's paper, were not discussed by him. It was recently said that

> in certain uses of these terms, and these perfectly legitimate uses, 'feeling sure' and 'knowing' are synonymous. I have just said that I feel sure that there are flowers in the garden, but I might equally well have said that I know that there are flowers in the garden and meant the same thing. In some contexts obviously to say that I feel sure is to say that I know.[1]

[1] R. I. Aaron, 'Feeling Sure', *Proc. Aristotelian Society*, Supp. Vol. XXX (1956), 2; cf. pp. 10, 12.

The conclusion that 'I know' and 'I feel sure' are sometimes synonymous is a mistake based on the quite correct point that we do not sincerely and justifiably put forward claims, and a fortiori claims to knowledge, unless we feel confident of their validity; therefore whenever we are prepared to say 'I know' we do feel confident, and vice versa. We might go further—and this is the second way in which a quite correct point may yet mislead us—and say that 'we should normally be prepared to express this complete confidence by saying that we *know* something to be the case'[1]. But it does not follow either from the fact that whenever we feel confident we are prepared to lay a claim, to say 'I know', or from the fact that a way of expressing our confidence is to say 'I know', that 'I know' and 'I feel sure' are synonymous, nor that it is logically self-contradictory to say, 'I know but I'm not very confident'. That it does not follow from the fact that confidence and claim-making go together is obvious enough. Because whenever I am drunk I start to sing and am prepared to promise anybody anything, and vice versa, it does not follow that 'I am drunk' means either 'I sing' or 'I promise'. There is an intimate connexion between 'I know' and 'I feel sure', but it is more causal than logical.

The difference between expressing complete confidence by saying 'I know' and describing it by saying 'I feel sure' is equally definite, though perhaps less obvious. To take a different kind of analogy: if I express my distaste for a person by saying, 'He's a horrid little man', this is not to *say* that I feel a distaste for him, and thus it is not synonymous with the description of my distaste, which might have been worded, 'I have a great distaste for him'. Similarly, to express my confidence by saying 'I know'—or for that matter by staking my reputation on the issue or doing any of the many other things which express confidence—is not to *say* that I feel confident; it is not to describe my attitude to the point. The analogy I have given here shows that this way of looking at the relation of 'I know' and 'I feel sure' is essentially the same as G. E. Moore's view that 'a man who asserted that Brutus' action was right in that sense would be *implying* that at the time of speaking he approved of it' in the sense that this is what he would normally be taken to be doing by using such language.[2] This also serves to show how the two mistakes I have mentioned are really based on the same correct point.

These differences between the synonymity of two expressions on

[1] L. E. Thomas, 'Philosophic Doubt', *Mind*, LXIV (1955), 335.

[2] *The Philosophy of G. E. Moore*, ed. by P. A. Schilpp (Evanstone, Ill., 1942), pp. 540–543 and elsewhere.

the one hand and the fact on the other either that the one expression describes something that usually, or even invariably, accompanies what is described by the other or that the one expression 'expresses' something 'described' by the other explain why it is more correct to say that certain sets of words are queer than to say that they are self-contradictory. I mean such sets as 'I know that so-and-so is the case, but I don't feel very sure about it' and 'I feel sure, but do I know?'

Again, if 'I know' and 'I feel sure' were ever synonymous, then what tended to prove that I did not know would tend to prove that I did not feel confident. This is patently false. What a disproof of 'I know' shows is neither that I was not confident nor that I was not reasonable in being so but that my confidence was misplaced, that my claim was invalid. When someone says 'I know so-and-so', and you ask 'Are you sure?', you are not asking him whether he really does know it, since often this cannot be decided at the moment, but whether he insists on making this claim, whether he is confident about it. This is the way in which some philosophers try to persuade us never to say that we know anything. They try to undermine our confidence so that we will make no claims.

The insistence that 'I know' makes a claim also helps, I think, to explain a point which has led some, e.g., Professor Norman Malcolm,[1] to suppose that there are two senses of 'know', namely, a strong and a weak. The point is that there are occasions on which we are sure we know, for instance that $2 + 2 = 4$ or that there is an ink-bottle in front of me, and others where we would admit an element of risk. Malcolm's solution is that we use 'I know that *p* is true' in a strong sense to mean that 'the person who makes the statement would look upon nothing whatever as evidence that *p* is false' and in a weak sense to mean that we would allow that something could prove it false. Now if it is correct that 'I know' makes a claim, Malcolm's strong sense would entail that we would be making a claim without allowing the possibility that it could be invalidated. But it is a logical characteristic of all claims that they may be validated or invalidated; it is a characteristic of all pretentions to knowledge that they may be exposed as fraudulent; of all confidence that it may be misplaced. I do not think that we ever do use 'know' in the way that Malcolm says we do. But a view very like Malcolm's may well be true and relevant. It is not that we do not *allow* or permit our claim to be invalidated, that we 'do not admit that my proposition could turn out to be false',

[1] 'Knowledge and Belief', *Mind*, LXI (1952), 178–189. [See p. 69 ff. of the present volume. Ed.]

but that we cannot *see* how the claim could be invalidated. That is why we assert 'I know' so strongly in these cases. It is a claim in which we place the utmost confidence because we cannot envisage what could upset it; it looks foolproof. I am perfectly justified in saying, 'I know that 2 + 2 = 4, that this is an ink-bottle'; there is nothing I could be more justified in saying, and it would be silly to suggest that I should be more modest or hesitant in my claim. But this is not because my claim could not be invalidated, that I do not allow it to be; it is because no reasonable man could be expected to see how it could and therefore could not be censured for making such a claim. This is the importance of Moore's appeal to common sense. He did not, I believe, mean so much that the statements of common sense were true or known to be true, but that whether they are or not—and he usually insisted that this could not be proved—it is more reasonable to claim them to be true, to claim we know them, than to make such a claim for any philosophical statement which contradicted them.

Furthermore, the distinction under consideration would, I believe, make better sense than Malcolm's does of the remarks of H. A. Prichard[1] on which he is commenting, namely, that we can by reflection discover whether we know or only believe something. First, we have to note that this remark is ambiguous, since the something in question may be one of a restricted set of examples or it may be anything at all. In the former case there is little difficulty. We say, for example, 'I know that my initials are A. R. W.; I don't just believe it'. Here, I suggest, we are emphatically prepared to make the claim to knowledge because that very claim has already been validated. We can have no fear that perhaps the courts will rule against it, because they have already ruled for it. But suppose that the something may be of any kind, for instance, that the Mycenean alphabet has twenty-seven letters. If I sincerely claim to know this, I cannot by reflecting on my condition discover whether I do know it or whether it is a false belief, and whether it is a valid or an invalid claim, for the claim has not yet been validated. But there is one interpretation which would make even the second sense of Prichard's remarks correct. If to say 'I know' is to make a claim, whereas to say 'I believe' is not, we can, merely by reflecting on our condition and without recourse to anything else such as the facts of the case, discover which we are doing, since this is only to discover

[1] *Knowledge and Perception* (New York, 1950), p. 88. [See p. 61 of the present volume. Ed.]

whether we are or are not making a claim. This fits in quite well with the revised version which Malcolm gives of his own view in *Analysis*.[1] He there says that instead of saying 'reflection can teach me that I know something in this [the strong] sense, what I should have said is that reflection can teach me that I am *using* "know" in the strong sense'. But it is misleading to put either Malcolm's or Prichard's point, on my interpretation of the latter, as discovering whether our condition is one of knowing or believing. If it is not put like this, but merely as I have suggested is the only correct way of putting it, then it ceases to be a matter of either dispute or interest.

Another recent article, which part of the time correctly emphasizes a distinction, though not the one I am considering, between 'I know' and 'He knows', arrives at a similarly mistaken conclusion.[2] The writer says, 'It is surely no harder in principle to discover by reflection whether we know something or not than to tell . . . whether we are merely sure that the prisoner will appear for trial or are willing to go bail for him'. This would be an apt comparison if what we were trying to discover was whether we were claiming to know or only believed something, but there is a world of difference between trying to discover whether we know and trying to discover whether we claim to know. The criterion of truth is relevant to the first in a way that it is not to the second.

The difference between the use of 'I know' to make a claim and the use of 'He knows' to allow it perhaps provides a clue to why people should have wished to say that knowledge is the limit or highest degree of belief, even while they realized that the criterion of truth is relevant to the former and not to the latter. 'He believes' and 'He knows' are vastly different, but there is much similarity between 'I believe' and 'I know', between announcing a belief and making a claim to knowledge. As the validity or invalidity of the claim is irrelevant to the reasonableness of making it, so the truth or falsity of the belief is irrelevant to the reasonableness of holding it. The same criteria, namely, good evidence and confidence, operate in judging the reasonableness of each.

It often seems only a character difference that leads some of us to say 'I believe' in circumstances where our bolder fellows would be prepared to lay a claim, to say 'I know'. We cannot be wrong in the way they can, nor can we be right; we cannot lose or win, since we have staked nothing. Sometimes we are more modest; at other times

[1] 'On Knowledge and Belief', *Analysis*, XIV (1954), 97.

[2] J. H. S. Armstrong, 'Knowledge and Belief', *Analysis*, XIII (1953), 117.

it is just that we do not have the courage of our convictions. Sceptical philosophy doth make cowards of us all. As our belief increases, so our willingness to claim is stronger. In this way claiming to know is closely related to a high degree of belief. The same sorts of things are said about beliefs and claims. Both can be stupid, obstinate, passionate, and groundless; or sensible, hesitant, calm, and well-supported. We ask what makes a person believe or claim to know; what makes him say he knows it, not what makes him know it. We ask *why* he believes, or claims to know, but we ask *how* he knows. Holding beliefs and making claims are things we tend to do, but we do not tend to know.

The reason for Woozley's denial of a difference in operation between 'I know' and 'He knows' lies, I think, not in any failure to see how 'I know' works, since its claim-making role is his main point, but in a failure to see that 'He knows' is used to allow, endorse, or favourably judge a claim. He speaks as if when *B* says of *A*, 'He knows so-and-so', what *B* is doing is to claim that *A* knows, whereas what in fact *B* is doing is to allow *A*'s claim. It is this difference that makes it clear why there is no difficulty in the fact that, while 'I'm sure, but do I know?' is queer, there is nothing at all wrong with 'He's sure, but does he know?'. In the first we are in the strange position that the claimant is making his claim and at the same time is trying to judge it as well, and this is what we cannot ordinarily do. We cannot normally act the part of vehement claimant and impartial or doubting judge at the same time. When the claimant is another, it is easy to assess his claim coolly. This is also why 'I *was* very sure about that at the time, but did I know it?' is like 'He's sure but . . . ' and not like 'I *am* sure but . . . '. We are not trying to judge the claim at the time we make it.

Of course, there is a rather strained sense in which a judge can be said not merely to pass a judgement but to claim that it is a valid one; or better, that in giving such a judgement he is implying, in the Mooreian sense, that he is prepared to claim it to be valid. In this way, perhaps, we could say that when *B* allows *A*'s claim to knowledge he is also claiming that *A* knows, and therefore we could apply the criteria of claims to *B*'s remarks as well as to *A*'s; we can say, '*B* might be able both truly and justifiably to say that *A* knew that *p*'.[1] This is also part of the explanation of the worry that in saying Brown's confidence does not prove his claim, we rely on our own confidence.[2]

[1] Woozley, op. cit., p. 153. [p. 84. Ed.]

[2] Aaron, op. cit., p. 8.

But even if a claim is implied, in this sense, in a judgement, as it may be implied in any assertion, the judgement is itself not a claim. 'I know' is used to make a claim, not to allow it; 'He knows' to allow it, not to make it. We do, of course, often make claims on behalf of another, and the appropriate words for this are 'He knows'. But here 'He knows' is, in a way, *oratio obliqua* for the claim which he would have expressed, had he made it, as 'I know'.

A reason why many people fail to see the difference in operation between 'I know' and 'He knows' is that they sometimes do operate in the same way. They are both often used merely to state a fact. This seems to be true of all language about claims. 'It is mine' or 'I am the heir to the Tredgold millions' may be used equally to make a claim or to state a fact, just as 'It is his' or 'He is the heir . . . ' are used either to allow his claim or to state a fact. Woozley clearly recognizes the claim-making role of 'I know' and, therefore, should not be misled by the above point, yet perhaps he is. For a ground of his view that the different forms of the verb are being used in the same way is that they both make the same statement about a person. In their fact stating use they admittedly do; but whether it is sensible or not to call judging a man's claim—which we do by using 'He knows'—making a statement about him, it is certainly not sensible to say that making a claim—which we do by using 'I know'—is making a statement about oneself.

A plausible objection to the view that 'He knows' endorses a claim or judges it favourably is that we often use this expression of someone when he has not, and in the circumstances would not have, made any claim. The answer to this lies partly in the admission that 'He knows', as also 'I know', occurs often in contexts where the whole idea of claims is out of place and partly in the following parallel. Professor Ryle has pointed out the logical differences of what he calls 'task' and 'achievement' words, the latter denoting the successful accomplishment of whatever is mentioned by the former, e.g., looking and finding, shooting and scoring, working and succeeding. But, as he admits, there are cases of success which are due to luck and cases where the success is not prefaced by any task performance. Here we are, I think, uncertain whether to call these achievements or not. Is arriving at a true conclusion without having weighed the evidence an achievement or not? Similarly, do we want to talk of judging or allowing a claim which has not been made; do we want to say that someone knows something when he does not say, or perhaps even believe, that he does? When philosophers discuss the criteria of knowledge, they explicitly consider claims to knowledge and not those cases where no claim has been made.

In a way, then, Woozley's main mistake lies in his apparent assumption that words operate in certain ways, whereas the truth is that people operate or fail to operate in certain ways with them. To discover the logic of language is to find out how words are used and not how they behave, much less what they look like. To label all uses of a set of words 'making a statement' is in one sense perfectly correct, but it conceals all that is important about them, as does the use of schematic forms like '*A* knows (that) *p*'. It is perfectly true that if *A* says, 'I know the date of the battle of the Boyne' and *B* says, 'You don't', then '*B* is denying exactly what *A* is asserting'; just as when *A* says, 'It's a man' and *B* says, 'It isn't'; or when *A* says, 'It's beautiful' and *B* says, 'It isn't'; or when *A* says, 'It's exciting' and *B* says, 'It isn't'; or when *A* says, 'The inheritance is mine' and *B* says, 'It isn't'; or when *A* says, 'I'm in pain' and *B* says, 'You're not'. In all these cases it is both true and important to insist that *B* is contradicting *A*. But it is more important not to say it, because we will then go on to examine how claims are related to their rejections, assertions of fact to their denials, judgements of value to their opposites, individual psychological reports to each other, and expressions of pain to their reports.

Woozley's important distinction between the justifiability and the validity—what he calls the truth—of a claim points to the fact that there are two ways in which we may judge a claim and, correspondingly, two sets of criteria by which we judge it. To say 'He knows' is a correct way of giving a judgement only when it is about the validity of the claim. Thus we say that people in the fifteenth century did not know and could not have known that the earth was flat because it is not flat, even when we allow that they might have been justified in saying that they knew. Whether the claim is justifiably made or not is irrelevant to whether we are to say 'He knows'.

If, however, what we wish to judge is the justifiability of making the claim, the reasonableness of the claim, the sort of phrase we use is 'He (you) would be (was) correct (justified) in saying he (you) knew'. To allow that his claim was a reasonable one to make is to allow that he was correct to say he knew, to use the words 'I know'. The contrast between the ways of expressing the two kinds of judgements about claims can be seen perhaps even more clearly in the ways we judge them adversely as unreasonable and invalid. To reject a claim as invalid we say, 'You couldn't have known because . . . '; to reject it as unreasonable, we say, 'You shouldn't have said you knew because (when) . . . .'

Though the sentence 'He (you) would be (was) correct (justified) in saying he (you) knew' is the appropriate one to allow the reasonableness of the claim, it is sometimes used to allow its validity. I believe this ambiguity is one of the reasons the distinction between claiming to know and knowing was not emphasized before. Because in one sense it is correct to argue that a person who does not know can never be right in saying 'I know', it has not been seen that in another sense a person who does not know—provided, of course, that he is not aware of this—can quite rightly say 'I know'. This is a reason why all the criteria relevant to knowledge were lumped together.

For a somewhat similar reason it is easy to see why the criterion of good evidence should have been thought to be relevant to the assessment of the validity of a claim when it is really relevant to the assessment of its reasonableness. We say, '*How* do you know?' but '*Why* do you claim to know?' Part of the answer to the second question—one of the criteria of the reasonableness of claims—consists in producing the evidence for the claim. But this also answers the first question. Yet I think its relation to the one question is different from its relation to the other. Both questions admit something—the first that you do know, the second that you have made a claim. Each arises only after an admission. But while to make the first admission is to admit the validity of the claim, to make the second is not to admit its reasonableness. Therefore, *ex hypothesi*, the first question *cannot* be relevant to the validity of the claim, whereas the second question *can* be relevant to the reasonableness of the claim. In this way a demand for evidence is a demand for a criterion of the reasonableness and not of the validity of the claim; it is relevant to the claim-making, not the claim. In regard to the claim itself, it is a demand for further information. So we often say, 'By the way (incidentally), how did you know?' But this further demand is one which is often included in the demand about the claim's validity. As Professor J. L. Austin points out, 'Do you know'? is 'commonly taken as an invitation to state not merely *whether* but also *how* we know'.[1]

There is another way in which the criterion of good evidence may perhaps be relevant not only to the justifiability but also to the validity of a claim to knowledge. To claim to know that so-and-so is the case is to claim possession of a truth, to claim to know how to do something is to claim possession of an ability or skill, to claim to know a

[1] 'Other Minds', *Proc. Aristotelian Society*, Supp. Vol. XX (1946), 149.

person or place is to claim possession of an acquaintance. Such claims can therefore be invalidated in two respects, namely, by the nonexistence of what is said to be possessed and by the nonexistence of the claimant's possession of it. Out of all this, the criterion of good evidence could be relevant only to the alleged possession of a truth. Did he know it, really possess it, or did he only guess it? Even here, as Moore has stressed, this criterion is of restricted relevance. First, there must be some things which are allowed to be known without our knowing the evidence; otherwise nothing could be known. Second, even where it is permissible to ask for evidence, it is a commonplace that we often admit that people know things for which they cannot give any reason at all. Besides, there are as many, and the same kind of, ways of finding out whether people know that so-and-so is the case or only guess it as there are of finding out whether they know how to do so-and-so or merely succeed by luck. Philosophers have paid so much attention to our ability to give the evidence for the truth of what we claim to know partly because they have overlooked these points and partly because they are more interested in how we know than in whether we know.

In general, judgements about the reasonableness of a claim are not always kept distinct from judgements about its validity. When law courts are assessing the validity of a claim they often at the same time pass judgement on the reasonableness of the claimants in bringing it and may award costs accordingly. It is not surprising that the criteria for the two kinds of judgement coalesce. Nor is Woozley himself free from worry on this point. 'I have,' he says, 'in my own mind, wavered between two versions of 'I think I know that' as = (1) 'I think my reasons for saying that are sufficient' or (2) 'I think my reasons for saying I know that justify saying I know that.' (1) is the version I have used. I am not sure that (2) isn't correct.' If I understand this, (1) would be a qualified judgement of the validity of a claim and (2) a qualified judgement of the reasonableness of a claim. The worry would then be whether the criterion of good evidence is relevant to the former or the latter judgement. This indecision appears throughout Woozley's paper. For instance, in one place he says 'whether my reasons for saying that I know that it is the case are good reasons' is a criterion of the justifiability of making a claim; in another he says that 'that I have sufficient reasons for asserting *p*, and that if I do assert *p*, I assert it for these reasons' is a criterion of the validity of the claim.

I do not wish to say that 'I know' is always used to make a claim—

or 'He knows' to judge it. Besides its use to state a fact, which we have seen that it has in company with other phrases used for claim-making, it is used, for example, to make admissions of difficulties, to announce the coming to a decision, to agree and commiserate, to make concessions, and in many other ways. Austin has suggested that it is used also to give one's authority, to give one's word, for saying so-and-so.[1] But it is its relation to claims to knowledge, to the notions of confidence, evidence, and truth, which has been the chief preoccupation of philosophers. It is because I believe that Woozley's distinction between claiming to know and knowing is illuminating for this that I have ventured these addenda and corrigenda. I feel further that a detailed investigation into the logic of claims would greatly help some of the problems of knowledge.

[1] Op. cit.

VIII

KNOWING AND PROMISING

JONATHAN HARRISON

PART I

INDEPENDENT TREATMENT OF THE SUBJECT

I

IN Part I of my paper, I shall be concerned only with the following types of sentence. I shall be concerned with sentences such as 'I know she will be late', said by Jones of Miss Robinson at time $t1$, and sentences such as 'Jones knew she would be late', said by Smith of Jones at time $t2$, and with sentences such as 'I promise not to be late', said by Miss Robinson at time $t1$, and sentences such as 'She promised not to be late', said by Smith of Miss Robinson at time $t2$.

I shall not be concerned with sentences where the verb 'know' (or 'knows' or 'knew') is not followed by a form of words such as 'she will be late' or 'that she will be late'. This means that I shall not be concerned with sentences where the word 'know' or 'knows' or 'knew' is followed by words or phrases such as 'his (or my) way', 'his (or my) onions', 'Birmingham', 'the Lord's Prayer', 'how to play contract bridge', 'how the internal combustion engine works',[1] 'where she is', 'why it's not going', 'when she will come', 'what the matter is', 'not to eat peas with my knife', 'the difference between margarine and butter'. The difference between those occurrences of 'know' with which I shall, and those with which I shall not, be concerned, is that with the former, but not with the latter, the words following 'know' express something

From *Mind*, Vol. 71 (1962), pp. 443–57. Reprinted by permission of the author and the Editor of *Mind*.

[1] 'Knowing how' must not be confused with 'knowing how to', though it is perhaps unnecessarily pedantic to point out that what is normally referred to as 'knowing how' would be more accurately described as 'knowing how to'. Knowing how the internal combustion engine works, for example, probably does only involve knowing that certain things about the working of the internal combustion engine are true.

capable of being true or false. It makes sense to say 'It is true (or false) that she is late', but it does not make sense to say 'Birmingham is true (or false)' or 'How to play contract bridge is true (or false)'.

Nor shall I for the moment be concerned with those cases where the word 'promise' (or 'promises' or 'promised') is followed by words like 'that she will not be late'. I am not suggesting that there is necessarily an important difference between promising to and promising that, but there may be, and when I promise that something will happen, over which I have, and know I have, and am known by my hearers to have, no control, there almost certainly is such a difference. I cannot break or keep this promise.

II

I think that, until fairly recently, most philosophers would have taken for granted the following things about what anyone who said 'I know she will be late' was doing.

(i) It would have been taken for granted that he was making a statement, or asserting a proposition, or saying something which could be true or false.

(ii) It would have been taken for granted that the proposition asserted by someone who said 'I know she will be late' was a different proposition from the one he would have asserted had he simply said 'She will be late'. It would have been taken for granted that if the former proposition were true, the latter proposition would have to be true too, but it would also have been taken for granted that the latter proposition could be true, but the former false.

(iii) It would have been taken for granted that when Jones said, at time t_1, 'I know she will be late', he was asserting the same proposition as that asserted by Smith, at time t_2, when he says 'Jones knew she would be late'. That is to say, it would have been taken for granted, not only that both Jones and Smith were saying something which had a truth-value, but that what they were saying must have the same truth-value; that Jones could not be saying something true, and Smith be saying something false, and vice versa.

(iv) It would also have been taken for granted that at least one problem involved in 'the problem of knowledge' was to say just what Jones was asserting about himself, when he said things like 'I know she will be late', and just what Smith was asserting about Jones, when he says 'Jones knew she would be late'. Briefly, it seemed natural to suppose that, since there were some true propositions which Jones knew, and others which he did not, the difference between his knowing some and not others lay in Jones; in what might, very inadequately, be called Jones's 'mental attitude' to these propositions, or his 'state of mind' concerning them. Again, since there were some true propositions which Jones knew, and others which he only believed, it seemed natural to suppose that the difference between Jones's knowing some true propositions, and only believing others, lay in Jones, again, in his 'state of mind' concerning them, or his 'mental attitude' towards them.

III

If what Jones is doing when he says 'I know she will be late' is like what Miss Robinson is doing when she says 'I promise not to be late', then all these traditionally made assumptions are wrong.

(i) When Miss Robinson says 'I promise not to be late', she is not saying something which can be intelligibly said to be true, or intelligibly said to be false. If Miss Robinson were to say to Smith, 'I promise not to be late', it would be improper for him to reply, 'That's true' or 'That isn't true', 'I agree' or 'I don't agree' or 'You must be mistaken'. If Smith were to say any of these things, it would show that he had misheard, or failed to understand, what Miss Robinson had said. Hence, if 'I know . . . ' is like 'I promise . . . ', anyone saying 'I know . . . ' will not be saying anything capable of being true or false, nor will he be capable of being mistaken.

(ii) If anyone saying 'I know she will be late' is not making a statement at all—and, if 'I know . . . ' is like 'I promise . . . ', he will not be—any question concerning the logical relations between the statement he is making, and the statement he would have been making if he had detached the words following 'know', viz. 'she will be late', from the whole sentence, and asserted them independently, does not arise. It is worth pointing out that it is natural to suppose that such a problem does arise in the case of 'I know . . . ', though not at all natural to suppose it arises in the case of 'I promise . . . ', for the words following 'know' could, in other contexts, express something capable of being true or false, but the words following 'promise' could not.

(iii) Since Miss Robinson, when she says at time t_1, 'I promise not to be late', is not making a statement, it is clear that she cannot be making the same statement that Smith makes at time t_2 when he says, 'Miss Robinson promised not to be late'. Hence, if 'I know . . . ' is like 'I promise . . . ', Jones, when he says, at time t_1, 'I know she will be late', cannot be making the same statement that Smith is making when he says at time $t2$, 'Jones knew she would be late'.

(iv) Again, since Miss Robinson, when she says 'I promise not to be late', is not making a statement, she cannot be making a statement about herself, and any one who supposed that this sentence asserted the occurrence of some 'mental act', which actually was the promising, which the sentence 'I promise not to be late' described, and tried to give an account of this act, would be chasing a will-o'-the-wisp. Hence, anyone asking what the special 'state of mind' Jones must be in when he truly says 'I know she will be late' will, if 'I know . . . ' is like 'I promise . . . ', also be chasing a will-o'-the-wisp.

IV

What Miss Robinson is doing when she says 'I promise not to be late', however, differs very considerably from what Jones is doing when he says 'I know she will be late', and in the following ways.

(i) When Miss Robinson says 'I promise not to be late', she has committed herself to doing something, i.e. to arriving on time, but she has not committed herself to any proposition's being true. When Jones says 'I know she will be late', however, he has committed himself, at the very least, to the proposition 'She will be late'.

(ii) Hence, if it turns out that, after all, she is not late, Jones will have to admit that he was wrong. There is no future eventuality, however, which could make Miss Robinson say that what she said when she said 'I promise not to be late' was wrong. Saying that something is wrong, of course, must not be confused with saying that somebody is wrong to say that thing; it can be wrong—and even a criminal offence—to say many things which are not wrong, and it can certainly be wrong *to say* 'I promise . . . '.

(iii) From the fact that what Jones says when he says 'I know she will be late' can be wrong, I am inclined to infer that it can have a truth-value. It must take the truth-value 'false', if she is not in fact late. Indeed if Jones said 'I know she will be late' when he knew perfectly well she would not be late, then what he said will not only be false, it will also very probably be the case that he is lying. Miss Robinson, on the other hand, when she says 'I promise not to be late' cannot be saying what is false, and cannot be lying. What is vulgarly called a 'lying promise' is not a lie, but a promise which one has no intention of keeping.

(iv) Can 'I know she will be late' be false, even if she is in fact late, as has always, until recently, been assumed? I am inclined to think it can, and for the following reason. Smith may perfectly well know that Miss Robinson was late, and yet not be convinced that Jones knew she would be, even though he is quite convinced that Jones said 'I know she will be late'. He may even be quite convinced that Jones did not know she would be late, even though Jones said 'I know she will be late', and she was late. It seems to me that, if Smith is right in thinking that Jones did not know she would be late when he said he did, even though she was late, then what Jones said must be wrong, and, if it was wrong, I am inclined to think it must have been wrong by being false. If this is the case, then what Jones is saying when he says 'I know she will be late' can be false, even though it turns out that she is late.

(v) The above argument, of course, assumes that what Smith says at time $t2$, viz. 'Jones did not know she would be late', is incompatible with what Jones says at time $t1$, viz. 'I know she will be late', for it reasons that since what Smith says is obviously capable of being true, even if she is in fact late, then what Jones says must be capable of being false in the same circumstances. This is just one of the very assumptions which will be invalid if 'I know . . . ' is like 'I promise . . . ', for what Miss Robinson says when she says 'I promise not to be late', is certainly not incompatible with what Smith says when he says 'Miss Robinson did not promise not to be late'. The fact that Miss Robinson has said this, of course, is a very strong reason—though not a conclusive reason, for she might, for example, have been joking—for thinking that Smith is wrong, but this does not mean that what she says is incompatible with what Smith says; at most the statement that she has said these words is incompatible with what Smith says. This is because one of the things which can make Smith's statement true is Miss Robinson's saying these words. One way—though not the only, or even the usual, way of promising—is to say 'I promise . . . ' in certain standard circumstances, e.g. in a language where these words have this function conventionally allotted to them, without the speaker winking, with knowledge of what he is saying, and understood by his hearer, etc. If these words have been said, and there is nothing to make saying them misfire, then Miss Robinson has promised. Her promising is not something over and above her saying these words, some mental act, for example, which these words are about, and the occurrence of which would make what she says true, and the non-occurrence of which would make what she says false. It is, as is sufficiently well recognized, just the saying of the words 'I promise . . .', and if she has said them, and the standard conditions are fulfilled, then Smith's statement 'Miss Robinson promised she would not be late' must be granted. But no-one could possibly maintain that what Smith says when he says 'Jones knew she would be late' is made true simply by the fact that Jones said the words 'I know she will be late'. One way of promising is just saying 'I promise . . . ', but saying 'I know . . . ' is not any way of knowing. Hence what Jones says when he says 'I know she will be late', and what Smith says when he says 'Jones knew she would be late' are not related in anything like the way in which what Miss Robinson says when she says 'I promise not to be late' is related to what Smith says when he says 'Miss Robinson promised not to be late'. This being so, there is no reason for supposing that they are not related in the way in which everybody, until recently, supposed they were related; no reason for supposing that what Jones and Smith are saying are not logically equivalent. If they are logically equivalent, then, since what Smith says when he says 'Jones knew Miss Robinson would be late' can be false, even though Miss Robinson was actually late, then what Jones says when he says 'I know she will be late' can also be false in the same circumstances, and what Jones says will not only have a truth-value, but a different truth-value from 'Miss Robinson will be late'.

(vi) If 'I know she will be late', said by Jones at time *t*1, is capable of being true or false, and can be false independently of Miss Robinson's being late, it seems not unnatural to suppose that the reason for all this is that it is a statement about Jones, in the sense that at least one of the things relevant to its truth is something about Jones. Jones is, in fact, saying about himself precisely what Smith is saying about him when Smith says at time *t*2 'Jones knew Miss Robinson would be late'.

(vii) The arguments I have used do not show that, when Jones says 'I know Miss Robinson will be late', he is not engaging in a performance over and above the performance of saying the words 'I know Miss Robinson will be late'. All it shows is that, if he is engaged in a performance, it is not a performance which is described by Smith when he says 'Jones knew Miss Robinson would be late'. In this respect, then, saying 'I know . . . ' is unlike saying 'I promise . . . ', but it may nevertheless be like saying 'I promise . . . ' in that anyone saying it is engaged in a performance, though not a performance which the words 'He knew . . . ' describe or assert to have occurred. Jones, when he says 'I know . . . ', may be staking his reputation, licensing others to argue or behave in certain ways, giving others his authority for saying certain things, even though someone saying 'Jones knows . . . ' is not saying that he is doing any of these things. I do not wish to deny that he is doing any of these things, though I doubt whether any of these descriptions of what he is doing are very helpful. But does it follow from the fact that he is doing these things that he is not doing what everyone, until recently, assumed he was doing, viz. making a statement about himself? It seems to me that this does not follow. To take examples from a different sphere, when I say that Thompson is a very good man, I may, I suppose, be described as commending him; when I say that a loaf is of the very best bread, I may, I suppose, be described as evaluating or appraising it; when I say that what Atkinson did was wrong, I may be condemning his action; when I say that Richardson is a bounder I may, to put it mildly, be described as expressing an unfavourable or con-attitude to him. It does not, however, follow from the fact that these descriptions of these men and this action are applicable, that what I am doing when I say these things does not consist in saying something capable of being true or false, any more than from the fact that what I am doing may consist in, say, reassuring someone, it would follow that I was not saying something capable of being true or false. Similarly, one way, though not the only way, of, say, staking one's reputation may be to make a certain statement about oneself, the statement that one knows such-and-such to be the case.

V

The upshot of this is that the suggestion that 'I know . . . ' is like 'I promise . . . ' is, at the very least, extremely misleading. I would not personally like to say that there was no resemblance between them, but it seems clear that the differences are more obvious and more important than the resemblances. One of the most important differences is that someone saying 'I promise . . . ' is thereby promising, whereas someone saying 'I know . . . ' is not thereby knowing, but simply claiming that he knows. Hence, though the question whether he really has promised may turn on the question whether he has said 'I promise . . . ', and not on the question whether what he said when he said 'I promise . . .' is a true statement about himself, the question whether he really knows does not turn on whether he has said 'I know . . .', but on whether, having said 'I know . . .', he has said something about himself which is true. If this is so, then past philosophers have not been chasing a will-o'-the-wisp when they asked 'In what condition must someone be who correctly says that he knows something, for his claim that he knows to be justified?'—or, at any rate, one reason for thinking they have been doing this is seen to be invalid.

VI

The above argument has been concerned with sentences like 'I promise not to be late', and not with sentences such as 'I promise that I will not be late'. Perhaps it would be as well to consider to what extent what has been said about 'promising to' applies to 'promising that', and to what extent it does not.

Sometimes one says 'I promise to . . .' when one might just as well have said 'I promise that . . . '. Whether Miss Robinson says 'I promise not to be late' or 'I promise that I will not be late', Smith can, in either case, say of her either 'Miss Robinson promised not to be late' or 'Miss Robinson promised that she would not be late'. In such cases I believe there is no important difference between 'promising to' and 'promising that', though in one respect 'promising that' resembles saying 'I know . . . ' more closely than does 'promising to'; in both 'I promise I will not be late' and 'I know I will not be late' the words following 'promise' and 'know' respectively could, in other contexts, be used to assert something capable of being true or false. However, both 'promising to' and 'promising that' are essentially different from saying 'I know . . . ', in that someone who says either 'I promise not to be late' or 'I promise that I will not be late' is correctly described as having promised, but someone saying 'I know . . . ' is not correctly described as having known.

There are, however, cases when someone says 'I promise that . . . ' when he could not just as well have said 'I promise to . . . ' Mrs. James can say 'I promise that Tommy will not be late', when it is not clear just how what she says could be paraphrased in terms of 'promising to'. Perhaps what she means is 'I promise not to let Tommy be late', but this is dubious, for she may feel sufficiently confident of Tommy's punctuality to be able to promise that he will not be late, without feeling that it will be necessary for her to take any steps to see that Tommy is not late. Indeed, sometimes when someone says 'I promise that . . . ' there are no steps which he could take, or could be taken to see that the eventuality promised occurs, as when, for example, the

Astronomer Royal says 'I promise that there will be an eclipse of the sun at 21.07 tomorrow'. In such cases 'promising that' is increasingly different from 'promising to'. It is, nevertheless, still unlike saying 'I know . . .', for the question whether the Astronomer Royal promised there would be an eclipse is settled by a consideration of what he said, i.e., of whether he said 'I promise that there will be an eclipse . . .', but the question whether or not he knew there would be an eclipse is not settled by a consideration of what he said.

PART II

PROFESSOR AUSTIN ON 'I KNOW' AND 'I PROMISE'

'Attacking men of straw' is an exercise which sometimes is philosophically enlightening. Since, however, there are some who have a prejudice against criticizing views which have never been held, it may be as well to consider to what extent the late Professor J. L. Austin thought that 'I know . . . ' resembles 'I promise . . . ' in ways in which these two do not resemble one another.[1]

I

Austin maintained that to suppose 'that "I know" is a descriptive phrase, is only one example of the *descriptive fallacy*, so common in philosophy' (p. 146). I am not sure what the 'descriptive fallacy' is, however. If the 'descriptive fallacy' is simply the fallacy of supposing that 'I know she will be late', like 'She is habitually unpunctual', and unlike 'Twice two are four', 'Dodos no longer exist' or 'The Battle of Hastings was fought in 1066', describes something, then Austin would certainly be right, but I doubt whether this contention, though true, would be relevant and important, or was the one he wished to make. If, however, the 'descriptive fallacy' is the fallacy of supposing that the function of certain words is to make a statement, expressing some truth or falsehood, when they have some other function, then my arguments do tend to show that Austin was wrong, and words like 'I know . . . ' do express a statement.

II

Perhaps the 'descriptive fallacy', however, lies in supposing, not that the sentences like 'I know *p*' do not convey something capable of

[1] *Logic and Language* (ed. A. G. N. Flew), 'Other Minds', pp. 142–147.

being true or false, but that putting 'I know' in front of any sentence does not alter the truth-value of what is being said, much as putting 'I warn you that' in front of 'The bull is going to charge' does not alter the truth-value of what is being said. Austin does not say that this is the way in which the words 'I know' are not descriptive, but he does himself mention 'I warn', etc., very shortly after saying that 'I know' is not a descriptive phrase (p. 145), and it is possible that he did think that the function of 'I know' was like the function of 'I warn'. If he did think this, then he was mistaken, for, though 'I warn you that the bull is going to charge' does not have a different truth-value from 'The bull is going to charge', 'I know that the bull is going to charge' does have a different truth-value from 'The bull is going to charge'. When said by Jones, 'I know the bull is going to charge' has the same truth-value as 'Jones knows the bull is going to charge', said by Smith. The view that adding 'I know' to 'The bull is going to charge' does not alter the truth-value of what the latter asserts has been more explicitly held, if I am not mistaken, by Mr. Urmson.[1] The above argument seems to me clearly to dispose of it.

III

It is clear that, if anyone were to suppose that the function of sentences like 'I promise . . . ' was to make an assertion about the speaker, he would be making a very serious error, and an error which could quite appropriately be described as a descriptive fallacy. Austin, immediately after having remarked that to suppose 'I know' is a descriptive phrase is to commit the 'descriptive fallacy', mentions 'obvious ritual phrases' such as 'I do' as examples of the non-descriptive use of language; when we say 'I do' we are not describing the action, but doing it (p. 147). Since, clearly, when we say 'I promise . . . ' we are also not describing the action, but doing it, and since Austin has likened 'I know' to 'I promise', it is at least possible that he thought 'I know' was non-descriptive in the way in which 'I promise' is non-descriptive. If he did think this, he was again mistaken, for, as I have already shown, though someone saying 'I promise' in the appropriate circumstances, is promising, not claiming to promise, someone saying 'I know' is simply claiming to know, not knowing. The temptation to the reader to suppose that Austin did think that 'I know' was like 'I promise' in this respect is very strong, so strong, indeed, that if he did not think so, it was quite extraordinary that he should not have pointed this out.

[1] 'Parenthetical Verbs', *Mind*, 1952.

IV

Austin himself points out one extremely important difference between 'I know' and 'I promise', viz. that someone who promises what he does not perform has, nevertheless, promised, though someone who says he knows something which is false cannot have known. He suggests, however, that this difference is 'more apparent than real. The sense in which you "did promise" is that you did *say* you promised (did say "I promise"): and you did *say* you knew' (p. 145). There is, however, according to Austin, another sense of 'promise' in which he who says 'I promise', but does not do what he promised, or did not fully intend to do what he promised, or promised what was not within his power, did not promise. In this sense of 'promise', promising and knowing are similar (145).

There is, however, only one sense of 'promise'; the only way of promising is to say 'I promise' (or use some other equivalent phrase or gesture) in the appropriate conditions. There is no sense in which someone, having said 'I promise' in these conditions, can be said, nevertheless, not to have promised. Hence there is no sense in which someone who promises what he does not intend, or what is outside his power, or who promises, but does not perform, has not promised. Indeed if there were, it would follow that there was a sense of 'promise' in which it was logically impossible to promise what you do not intend to, or what you cannot, or what you do not perform, from which it would follow that there was a sense of 'promise' in which it was logically impossible to break a promise, which is absurd. If you say 'I promise X' when you do not fully intend to do X, or cannot do X, or subsequently do not do X, then you may have been casual, inconsiderate, or immoral, but you have made a promise. Hence someone who claims to know something that is, in fact, false, only says 'I know', and does not in any sense know; someone who says 'I promise', but does not perform, not only says 'I promise', but promises and does not in any sense not promise.

Strictly speaking, Austin does not say that there is a sense of 'promise' in which he who promises but does not perform, etc., has not promised, but that there is 'a "sense" of promise' in which this is true. I do not understand the unexplained difference between a sense of 'promise' and a 'sense' of promise, especially when the latter is contrasted with a sense of 'promise' (and not a 'sense' of promise) in which he who promises, but does not perform, has promised.

V

Austin rightly suggests that sometimes the worry concerning whether Jones did promise, or order me, or marry his landlady, or warn me that the bull was about to charge, may be a worry concerning whether Jones, having said 'I promise' or 'I order you' or 'I do' or 'I warn you', said these words in the appropriate circumstances, or whether, because he winked, or had no authority, or was not in front of a real clergyman, or knew nothing about bulls, the appropriate circumstances did not all obtain, and so, though Jones did say 'I promise', etc., Jones cannot properly be described as having promised. He then says 'We hesitate between "He didn't order me", "He had no right to order me", "He oughtn't to have said he ordered me", just as we do between "You didn't know", "You can't have known", "You had no right to say you knew . . ."' (145–146). There is an enormous difference, however, between our worry concerning whether someone did warn, or order, or promise, or marry, and our worry concerning whether he knew. Our worry concerning whether he did warn, or order, or promise, or marry, is a worry concerning whether he, having said 'I warn', or 'order' or 'I promise' or 'I do', said these in the appropriate circumstances. But North's worry concerning whether East knows he has the King of Spades is not a worry concerning whether East, having said 'I know North has the King of Spades', said this in the appropriate circumstances. East can perfectly well know this, without *saying* anything at all.

VI

Austin suggests that if someone were to suppose that the difference between 'I promise' and 'I fully intend' was that promising is something higher in the same scale than fully intending, he would be mistaken. He also suggests that if someone thought that the difference between 'I know' and 'I believe' or 'I am certain' was that knowing was higher in the same scale than believing, he would be mistaken. If all he means is that someone who knows is not more certain of what he knows than someone who is merely absolutely certain, then he is surely right. There is nothing more certain than certain. But he may be suggesting that, just as someone would be mistaken who supposed that 'I promise' was a different and 'more extreme' statement about the speaker than 'I fully intend', so someone who supposed that 'I know' makes a different and 'more extreme' statement about the speaker than 'I am quite sure' would also be mistaken. It is clear that—supposing that one who says 'I fully intend' is making a statement about himself—to adopt the first course would be to make a mistake, and a bad one. The above arguments have shown, however, that to adopt the second course—supposing that one who says 'I am quite sure' is making a statement about himself—is not to make a mistake.

VII

Austin claims 'But the essential factors are (*a*) You said you knew: you said you promised, (*b*) You were mistaken: you didn't perform' (146). Here Austin has made knowing and promising appear more similar than they are, for he appears to suppose that 'You said you promised' parallels 'You said you knew'. This it does not. 'You said you knew' is indirect speech for 'You said "I know"', but 'You said you promised' is not indirect speech for 'You said "I promise"' but indirect speech for 'You said "I promised"'. Illegitimately substituting 'You said you promised' for 'You promised' or 'You said "I promise"', makes it possible for Austin to suggest that, just as you said you knew, but did not, because you were mistaken, so you said you promised, but could not have done, because you did not perform. But though you did not know what turned out to be false, you did promise what you did not perform, for all you need to do to promise is simply to say 'I promise' with a straight face, but a lot more is required to know than to say 'I know'.

VIII

Though it is not always entirely clear in what ways Austin thinks 'I know' resembles 'I promise', he is quite explicit on one point. Both someone who says 'I know' and someone who says 'I promise' give others their word (144). There are, however, cases when we would certainly not say of someone who said 'I know *p*' that he gave his word that *p*. If X says to me 'I know that you are determined to make a fool of yourself', he is surely not correctly described as having given me his word, pledged his authority, that I will make a fool of myself. When the amateur investigator says to the detective-inspector 'I know there is strong circumstantial evidence against him, but . . . ' it would be very odd to describe what he is doing in the way Austin does. In general, when X says to Y 'I know that *p*', when he believes Y to be already aware of *p*, he is not doing this so much to assure Y of *p*, as to communicate to Y the fact that he also knows *p*. In such cases, to describe X as giving his word to Y that *p* is true would be thoroughly implausible.

It is true that we could perhaps say that when X says to Y 'I know that *p*' when Y himself is not aware of the fact that *p*, we could describe X as giving his word to Y that *p*, and describe the situation which obtains when Y already knows *p* differently. X, however, may say 'I know the gun is loaded' both to Y, who knows this too, and to Z, who does not, but wants to know whether it is or not. In this case, he *may* be giving his word that the gun is loaded to Z, who is concerned about this, but he certainly cannot be described as doing this when he says the same thing to Y, who knows this already, and is only interested in whether X, too, knows. Since he is, presumably, saying the same thing to Y that he is saying to Z, and he is making a statement to Y, it follows that he is also making a statement to Z. Hence, even if it is correct to describe him as giving his word to Z, this description is not incompatible with his making a statement about himself. Even if Austin were sometimes right in thinking that someone saying 'I know *p*' is giving his word, he who says 'I know *p*' is, nevertheless, always also making a statement.

IX

But is Austin's description of what someone saying 'I know *p*' is doing ever true? Is it ever the case that someone saying 'I know *p*' is properly described as giving his word that *p*, etc.? I do not think that it is. Someone who says 'I give you my word that it isn't loaded', 'I guarantee it isn't loaded', 'I swear it isn't loaded', can properly be described as having given his word that it was not loaded, but someone who simply says 'I know it isn't loaded' cannot. He is doing, what the others are certainly not doing, stating a fact about himself. The effect of his stating this fact may be the same as the effect of his saying 'I swear the gun is not loaded'; someone does, or does not, pull the trigger, depending upon what it is they wish to achieve. Similarly, the purpose of someone who says 'I know the gun is loaded' may be the same as the purpose of someone who says 'I swear that the gun isn't loaded', viz. to cause someone to pull, or not to pull, the trigger, depending upon whether the speaker does, or does not, want the trigger pulled. This is because 'I know the gun is loaded' entails 'The gun is loaded' which may be what his hearer wants to know. But perhaps he already knows this, and wants to know whether the speaker knows this too. In this latter event, 'I swear the gun is loaded' would not do for giving Y the information he needs.

When the interesting and important discovery that language had other uses than to state facts, describe things, or communicate information was first made, it was only natural that philosophers should over-estimate the extent to which language was 'non-propositional' and the extent to which age-old philosophical problems had arisen as a result of the mistaken view that it was. The view that the function of 'I know' resembles the function of 'I promise' is a case in point. The discovery, largely due to Austin, that someone saying 'I promise' or 'I do' or 'I warn' or 'I name' or 'I take' was not making a statement about himself to the effect that he was in some special state, or undertaking some special performance, but actually, by saying these words, engaging in the performance, was both interesting and important. The assimilation of the more philosophically important words 'I know', however tentative or partial, to this class of words is just a mistake. Our predecessors, so far from committing the 'descriptive fallacy' with regard to 'I know', had the better of us in that they did not make this mistake.

IX

ON BELIEF

A. PHILLIPS GRIFFITHS

THERE will always be some conditions which must be presupposed in the claim that a certain concept is capable of application in judgements. In most cases, to claim that a judgement is correct presupposes that there is some particular satisfaction of these conditions. For example, to say that we can claim to make any correct judgements at all about physical objects requires that they should have causal relations to one another and to our sensibility. But, furthermore, to claim that some particular physical object can justifiably be said to exist is to presuppose that we can point to some particular satisfaction of these conditions: such as that we can see it, or that it has left a dent in the sand. I shall call concepts of which all this is true *a-concepts*.

But there are other concepts which can sometimes justifiably be applied in judgements where no particular satisfaction of the general conditions of the possibility of their application is claimed. For example, the concept 'pain' would not be capable of being applied in general as a concept of the public language unless there were some publicly determinable conditions, such as behavioural reactions, connected with being in pain. But I do not, in claiming to be able to say correctly that I am in pain, have to satisfy myself that any such publicly determinable conditions are satisfied. I shall call concepts of this second kind *b-concepts*.

In what follows I shall briefly try to rule out theories which treat 'belief' as an *a*-concept or an *a*-concept involving *b*-concepts; I shall then try to show that belief is a *b*-concept which is not reducible to other *b*-concepts; and finally I shall try to deal with the problem to which these claims lead.

From *Proceedings of the Aristotelian Society*, Vol. 63, (1962–3), pp. 167–186. Reprinted by courtesy of the author and the Editor of the Aristotelian Society.

To say that to believe is to act as if whatever one believed were true is to treat belief as an *a*-concept. I shall not spend much time on this. It has already been disposed of by Chisholm's arguments, in his book *Perceiving*, which I need not repeat. There is nothing against inventing a concept of 'belief' which is explicable entirely in terms of people's behaviour, but this would bear little relation to the concept ordinarily introduced by the term 'belief'. One thing must be obvious with regard to belief: it is connected in some way with thinking (itself a *b*-concept). People cannot be taken to believe things they have never heard of, or could not think.

However, there are two possible ways of treating belief as an *a*-concept which involves *b*-concepts. One is behavioural: the view that to believe *p* is to have a disposition, to act as if *p* were true in appropriate circumstances, given that *p* is thought of or could be thought of by the agent. Now only the assertion of an identity between my *voluntary* behaviour tendencies and my beliefs would be even remotely plausible. Furthermore, on this theory I will act in one way rather than another in a given situation because of the nature of my needs or wants. Now my voluntary behaviour is not the only behaviour explained by my wants: these would also explain some cases of blushing, trembling, belly-rumbling etc. Hence my wants cannot be regarded as constituted by my voluntary behaviour. What then is the connexion between my wants and my voluntary behaviour? It is not identity; it is not causality. What is it? The only remaining possibility which is plausible is that it is what I regard it as reasonable or advisable to do: that is, certain of my beliefs. The theory is therefore circular. A similar, and more immediate circularity, is to be found in the alternative way of trying to make belief into an *a*-concept: the view that belief, while requiring the *b*-concept of thinking or entertaining, requires also only the addition of the tendency to assert what is believed. This is immediately circular as it stands, since beliefs can be revealed only by *sincere* assertion, and a sincere assertion is surely nothing but an assertion which one believes to be true. Even if it is insisted that sincere assertion is not a special kind of assertion, but assertion *simpliciter*, whereas insincere assertion is assertion together with special factors which explain its distortion, the circularity is not avoided. For a man asserts what he believes in *what he believes are the appropriate circumstances*: and these in turn cannot be explained in terms of what he has a disposition to assert.

All these theories in their various ways suffer from a criticism which is a direct consequence of trying to represent belief as an *a*-concept. They both misrepresent my knowledge of my beliefs. I may know what I believe without knowing what I am going to assert; and I can have a tendency to assert something—in answering questions impatiently and carelessly, for example—which *I* at least know is not what I believe. This leads me to what I regard as centrally important to belief, and to something which is vital to my subsequent argument. In an indispensable sense of 'belief', some judgements of the form 'I believe *p*' are incorrigible. I am an authority on what I believe; I know what I believe, simply in virtue of believing it; and I cannot be mistaken about what I believe on every occasion. That this may be so I must now try to show.

It is of course very often possible to speak of a man as not knowing, or as being mistaken about, what he believes. A man might be said to have certain beliefs all his life which he never formulates to himself; a man may be said to have beliefs while he is asleep, or thinking of something quite other. The theories we have discussed fit these cases best; they claim that to say these things is to say that a man will do or say certain things in certain circumstances. But they fail because they ignore the cases where a man does actually have consciously before him what he believes. In these cases (which some might prefer to call cases of *judgements*) it is not possible to speak of a man as mistaken about what he believes; whereas, on these theories, it should be.

A man who did not believe that any of the apostles denied Christ might quite honestly and sincerely say 'I believe everything that is written in the Bible'. Such a man would not believe that there is any account in the Bible of one of the apostles denying Christ. His mistake about what he believes is not a mistake about what he is currently thinking about and not believing, but about something he is not currently thinking about. He is no more mistaken about what he has consciously in mind that he would be mistaken about what pains he has if he said 'I am feeling all the pains you just mentioned' where one pain had, without his knowledge, been just mentioned and which he did not feel.

Again, we may speak of a man as having believed something all his life which he never managed to formulate or bring to consciousness. One might dispute this, indeed, and say a more precise way of putting the matter is that the man would believe certain things *if* he formulated them or brought them to consciousness. But in any case, it by no means follows that a man may be mistaken about what he believes when he *has* formulated it or brought it to consciousness.

More difficult are those cases in which one actually denies a knowledge of one's own beliefs: for example when a man says 'I don't know what I believe about the hereafter'; but many of these cases seem to be ones not of belief but of doubt; as one might say equally well 'I don't know what *to* believe about the hereafter' or 'I can't quite make up my mind about the hereafter'. Professor Findlay has pointed out to me an even more difficult case; where a man says 'I believe in immortality' and, asked 'Why then are you so afraid of death?' and regarding his fear as incompatible with his belief—instead of sensibly reflecting that if there is no hereafter there is nothing to be afraid of—answers, 'Yes; perhaps I don't really believe in immortality'. The case is a strange one. The speaker seems to be standing back from himself and looking at himself as he would at another, applying to himself the same criteria of belief—in terms of action, assertion, etc.—that he would to another. It is like a man who, asked 'Will you marry the girl?' answers by considering the incidence of jilting in his social class, his previous bachelor-like tendencies, etc., instead of simply saying, 'That is my intention'. Another way of dealing with the question 'Do I really believe in immortality?' (given that I also believe that there is more to fear from extinction than from survival) is to say, 'If I do, my fear of death is pathological, to be explained by some ingrained associations or habits'; and then to look at the question of immortality and make up one's mind on it. The doubt about the belief may be that one has forgotten the compelling reasons for believing in it that one had, or perhaps that one never had any, and one is saying, 'Yes, perhaps if I look at the question squarely again I shall admit that there is no immortality: because whatever factors make me afraid to die will when taken properly into account also lead me to think nothing follows death except putrefaction'. At any rate, there is surely a difference between the neurotic pathological fear of a man on a high ladder who knows perfectly well that it will not give way and yet feels insecure, and the state of a man who for good or neurotic reasons actually believes the ladder will give way. Or again, a man might when drunk say with vehemence, 'The South Africans are obviously unfit for self-government and ought to be mandated to Nigeria', and be told 'You don't really believe that'. On sobering up he might admit that he did not believe it; but he might equally well say 'I don't believe it when I'm sober but I'm convinced of it when drunk'. One of the joys and dangers of being drunk is that all sorts of things which are normally difficult and complicated issues of doubt and questions turn into certain affirmations. Another case is where someone says, 'I believe in the theory of relativity' and is told 'You don't; you don't understand it'. The answer might be: 'Oh yes I do, and I believe it: I believe Einstein was right when he said beauty is in the eye of the beholder and what is morally right depends on local social conditions'. What the man is here mistaken about is what the theory of relativity is, not about what he believes. He believes what he is entertaining, but what he is entertaining is the product of a misunderstanding of what someone else has said. One knows what one believes in so far as one knows what one thinks, and one believes only so far as one thinks: but what one thinks may not in fact be expressed by or connected with what one says. It would seem that no convincing case can be found of being mistaken about whether one here and now believes something that one is currently thinking. The cases all seem to be one of misreporting beliefs, or of mistaking what one would believe on most occasions or in one's better moments; or of believing something at one time and not at others.

Now, if this is correct, and there are occasions on which 'I believe' is incorrigible, depending on the authority of the speaker, then 'belief' is a *b*-concept. It would seem that the only *b*-concepts for which we have application are those which are incorrigible only in the first person. But if there are to be any *b*-concepts at all, there must be the possibility of their application in a way which is completely dependent on authority; for if they are to be applicable while no particular conditions of their application need be satisfied, it must be the case that *someone* just *is* able to apply them. All this assumes however, that judgements in which the concept of belief are applied may be true when they are applied incorrigibly. But there appear to be concepts which, while they may be applied in judgements which are either true or false in the third person, are not so applied in first-person judgements. This is true of so-called 'performative' concepts. When I say 'I promise', that I have promised is dependent entirely on my authority, on my saying it, at least in normal cases. But on the other hand 'Is that true?' is not ordinarily a reasonable response to the remark 'I promise'.

Is it possible then that 'I believe' is performative? There is a certain difficulty in saying what a performative utterance is. However, for our purposes I think it will be enough if we define a performative utterance in terms of two factors which apply to the paradigm of all performative utterances: the locution 'I promise'. These are, first, that an utterance is performative if it is not a report of something one is doing, but the actual performance itself. This is too wide, since it would apply to every occasion of making a statement. It may however be narrowed by requiring, secondly, that no utterance is performative unless the fact of its utterance is sufficient for the truth of any statement constructed by changing only the person or the tense of the original utterance or any of its equivalents. Thus, while the utterance itself is the performance, the statements so formed will be true of the performance. For example if I say 'I promise to do *x*' this is sufficient for the truth of 'Griffiths promises to do *x*' or 'I promised to do *x*'. Now on this criterion it is clear that 'I believe' is not performative. Saying 'I believe' is not necessarily believing, and my saying 'I believe *p*' is not sufficient for the truth of 'Griffiths believes *p*' or 'I believed *p*'. To make a lying promise is to promise; to make a lying statement of belief is not to believe.

If 'I believe' is not performative, then there would seem to be no alternative to thinking that it is a report of something which is supposed to be the case: a statement of fact, which is known to the speaker without evidence or possibility of mistake. It is, then, a term which introduces a *b*-concept.

Now how can this *b*-concept, of belief, be explicated? Can it, for a start, be reduced to some other *b*-concepts? I shall now discuss what seem to me the only remotely plausible attempts to explain belief in terms of other *b*-concepts. There may be others, and they cannot be disposed of in advance; though it does seem plausible to say, on inspection, that there is nothing in common between the various cases of belief other than the entertaining of the proposition believed.

It has been suggested that to believe *p* is to entertain *p* and at the same time to have a feeling, the concept of which is a *b*-concept, such as a feeling of conviction, or a 'yes' feeling. Now this is simply factually false, if the feeling is supposed to be as obvious to the person that has it as is his belief. I am in many cases of belief unaware of such feelings. If I am now told that this is a result of my introspective ineptitude, and that if I were more skilful I should be able to detect such feelings, I shall reply that while this may be true, it constitutes an admission that we cannot regard belief as reducible to the presence of such feelings. For to apply the concept of belief completely adequately to myself, I need to know of no such feelings, even though I can apparently be brought to an awareness of them by training. I do not attribute beliefs to myself on a basis of my feelings, which are themselves distinct from beliefs. It could still be said that believing is having a feeling, because being in pain is having a feeling and I do not attribute pains to myself on a basis of my feelings—I feel my pains. But this would say nothing, for it does not explain belief in terms of any other concepts (for example, a feeling of conviction or safety) but merely classifies the unanalysable concept of belief as a concept of feeling. This does not damage the concept of belief, but it does a great deal of damage to the concept of feeling: it stretches it painfully.

Any attempt to reduce belief to entertaining *p* while having evidence for *p* must fail on two counts; first, because 'having evidence' must itself involve beliefs about the evidence, and secondly, because people undoubtedly believe things on many occasions without evidence at all. The Cook-Wilsonian account of this matter, however—for example, as it was put forward in a rather amended form by Price (*Aristotelian Society*, *Proceedings*, 1934–5)[1]—to some extent escapes these objections. For what we have been calling belief is on this theory distinguished into three quite different states of mind: knowledge, opinion, and taking for granted. Knowledge is what is directly presented to consciousness, about which there can be no mistake; hence 'having evidence' is explained in terms of knowledge, that is that what is given as evidence is the known. Opinion is entertaining a proposition, and having evidence for it; whereas taking for granted is believing something without doubt while one has no evidence for it. Thus, the concept belief has been reduced to three distinct concepts, and 'belief' means *either* knowledge *or* opinion *or* taking for granted.

But we need a concept of belief which is independent of these three. For we often attribute beliefs to people without any knowledge of how they came to acquire them or whether they can be justified. We may say that either these beliefs are formed on evidence or simply taken for granted; but we can identify them as beliefs and as more than mere entertaining without knowing which. But if there were no cognitive state here beyond mere entertaining except either opining or taking for granted, it would be impossible to know that someone believed something without first discovering that it was one rather than the other of the two.

Even if the concept of belief cannot be reduced to any other, it does at least presuppose the concept of entertaining. By entertaining, I do not merely mean understanding: understanding involves a relation to some given expressions, which one may understand or fail to understand; but entertaining a proposition may be misunderstanding

[1] [See pages 41–59 of this volume. Ed.]

another proposition. Entertaining is sometimes defined (e.g., by Price) as thinking of a proposition while not considering its truth, or not considering it true. I see no reason however to limit the concept of entertaining to propositions. Just as it is possible to understand commands, questions, or exclamations, it is possible also to entertain what one understands when one understands them. But it is impossible to believe anything without entertaining a *proposition*, that is to say, it is a condition of believing something that the person who believes should be willing to apply the concept of *truth* to what he believes. There can be no distinction between believing something and believing it to be true, and for every belief the words 'is true' can be added without further justification; and this of course applies to beliefs like '*p* is false': what is believed is that it is true that *p* is false. The object of belief must then be something capable of truth and falsity, such as 'There is no present King of France' or 'The present King of France is bald' or 'All squares have three diagonals'; it cannot be anything like 'Polly put the kettle on' or 'What is the time?' This does not mean that if a man says 'I believe that Polly put the kettle on' or 'It is my convinced opinion that what is the time', he thinks he has a belief and is mistaken: it means that what he says is, as it stands, unintelligible. Either he does not know what the word 'belief' means; or he does believe something such as that Polly is putting the kettle on, or that 'what' is a time between midnight and a minute past midnight, and that that is the time.

But in so far as the request, 'Polly put the kettle on' and the question 'What is the time?' can be understood, they can be entertained. The various modes of thought—including willing, wondering, and believing—are related to these various kinds of locution. To command something seriously, or seriously to accept a command addressed to oneself, is to will; to question seriously, and to accept a question without replacing it with a statement, is to wonder; to state something seriously, or to accept something seriously, is to believe. But entertaining a command is not willing, nor entertaining a question wondering, nor entertaining a statement believing. These are all concepts of possible modes of thought; but they are intelligible as concepts of the public language only in terms of the variety of objects, such as commands, statements and questions, which distinguish them. None of these objects is what it is apart from the use which a thinking being makes of it; on the other hand, how a thinking being thinks, what distinguishes the modes of his thought, requires for its description these various modes of speech. Thus, that one can believe only that which can be either true or false, and that one cannot believe what is a command or question, is no arbitrary linguistic convention about the meaning of the word 'believe'; it is rooted in the conditions under which it is possible to distinguish one mode of thought from another.

This does not, however, tell us *what* belief is; belief must involve entertaining a proposition, but it must be more than merely entertaining it; but that more cannot be understood in terms of truth, for while believing p is believing that p is true, equally, entertaining p is entertaining that p is true.

If anything is to be said to explain the concept of belief and its place among other concepts, then it cannot be that belief can be reduced to factors of the kind which fall under *a*-concepts; equally, while it presupposes other *b*-concepts, it cannot be reduced to other *b*-concepts. What other possibilities are there?

An account of belief has recently been published (in Findlay's *Values and Intentions*) which tries to avoid both these kinds of mistakes. Instead of trying to analyse belief in terms of other concepts, so that every case of belief is a case to which these concepts apply, it tries to show that all the disparate cases of belief can be held together as cases of belief by their relation to the full-blown, paradigm cases of belief which can be explicated in terms of other concepts. The paradigm case expresses the essence of belief; but this essence is not necessarily to be found in every particular case of belief, rather as the Platonic forms are only imperfectly reflected in particulars, or as the whole nature of a monad is only foreshadowed by its state at any one time.

The full cases of belief may be distinguished from mere entertaining in the following way, Findlay says. Generally speaking, the content of our entertaining—the meaning of something we assert as entertained for example—can be exhausted by a limited description. Thus, in entertaining the proposition that the cat is on the mat, I can be taken to be thinking no more than that an animal of a certain appearance is sitting on a covered bit of floor. In thinking this I think nothing about the condition of the air surrounding the cat, nothing about what the animal will do next, nothing about its origins; nor do I need to do so in order to grasp completely adequately what is meant by saying 'The cat is on the mat'. But if

I believe the cat is on the mat, I will be astonished to find that the temperature of the air surrounding the cat is a million degrees centigrade, or that there is no air in the room, or that the previous history of the cat is that of a dog, or that in a few moments the cat will get up and fly away. I cannot specify in advance all the ways in which conditions may surprise me if I believe that the cat is on the mat: but in believing I am ready to meet the non-surprising conditions rather than the surprising ones. Findlay puts it, 'I swallow with what I believe the absence of all the things which would disallow or exclude it, and am favourably disposed to all the things not otherwise disallowed that would bear favourably upon it, no matter how vague my conception of such circumstances may be'. Furthermore, I must be ready to match my belief against anything: I can rule out nothing as possibly relevant to it, and hence the system of belief must be an all-embracing system. It would of course be circular if this meant that belief is what we require to accord with other beliefs. Certainly our beliefs must do this, but they must initially and primarily fit in with and anticipate what Findlay calls the 'background of compulsive experience'—experience whose unavoidability is palpable, which means, for us, mainly, though not exclusively, sense-experience. Nor does this theory distinguish belief by its content: *what* is believed is the same as what is entertained: but in believing we are *also* ready to meet other beliefs and experience in a certain way.

Now, whether or not this is a convincing description of the most full-blown cases of belief, it is certainly not a description of very many actual cases of belief. One may believe things in the teeth of one's compulsive experience. Findlay says, 'while belief may be manifest in a wide range of impoverished, blunted and denatured forms, such as some analysts have loved to dwell upon, they only qualify for membership in the belief-family because of their graded approximation to a form which is, as it were, the fountain and origin of the whole set, which exemplifies belief in its most perfect form, as the finished portrait of which they are merely sketches'. Thus Tertullian, he says, 'may have believed something *because* it was absurd, but he could only do so because he and countless others had formed their beliefs less abnormally'.

Findlay cannot mean to deny that absurd beliefs, beliefs inadequately based, beliefs unconnected with one's other beliefs and which may even contradict them, are beliefs at all. It would be a mistake to say that they are quasi-beliefs. To those who have them they are as fully and completely beliefs as any others. They are not good beliefs, or desirable or sensible beliefs, but they are perfect beliefs in the sense that they undoubtedly count as beliefs. They are not all a belief should be, but they are what a belief is. Now what is the principle of unity which allows us to identify all these as beliefs? It is not that all these cases can be understood as coming under some other concepts, of an *a*- or *b*-kind. But Findlay's answer is that they all have a 'graded approximation' to the full case, the essence, he has described. There are two difficulties, of quite different kinds, in this.

First, how is the more unfavoured case of belief distinct from merely entertaining? It itself has none of the marks of the favoured case: then why is it a case of unfavoured belief, rather than not a case of belief at all? The only answer I could give that question is that its holder says it is a belief: that one knows when one believes, and this (together with the demand that what is believed is a proposition) is the absolutely apodeictic requirement that the concept makes. Yet the search for internal marks to distinguish all cases of belief is fruitless: there is nothing in common between beliefs that is not shared by non-beliefs, and Findlay's relation between unfavoured and favoured beliefs is not one that is perceived or indeed which even exists when the favoured kind of beliefs are not there. The only kind of position we can take is therefore that our knowledge of what we believe is not a knowledge of something with internal marks. How, then, *do* we know what we believe? The question seems demanded because we want to make all cases of knowing like those common public ones, where an object is discriminated and can be described. But not all cases of knowledge are like this. I do not know of my bodily movements by making inferences from physical sensation (cf. Anscombe, *Intention*, on this) but I do know (though I can be mistaken about) my bodily movements. I know of my intentions, and that I intend, without inspecting some quasi-substantial velleities. There is even something rather odd of speaking of knowing what my pains are like by inspecting their internal nature, rather than simply saying I have the pain or am in pain. All these cases are very different, and very different from belief: but their very differences should teach us not to force them, and the case of belief, into the single mould of perceptual discrimination of external objects. Belief is a discriminable mode of consciousness, but that does not mean that it must be discriminable in the way that a timbre or a dark streak on a wall is discriminable. It is discriminable in the way that modes of consciousness, such as doubting, willing, and wondering are all discriminable modes of consciousness, and this is something of its own sort.

My point is that if this account—or mere classification—of belief as a mode of consciousness is thought to say nothing and provide no answer, it is still preferable to the other theories discussed. For while the behaviourist theory provides a very clear and full answer, it is a false one, and if I say nothing, I at least say nothing false; whereas while I would not say that Findlay's answer is false, it too does not provide an answer. For the question, 'What tells me that any belief is a belief?' is not answered by saying, 'Because it somehow lives in a belief-family which is identified by its head'; what then marks the subordinate and unfavoured cases as members of the belief family? Certainly neither consanguinity nor legal adoption.

My second objection to Findlay's theory is that it is, if true, only a detailed and articulated insight: that is, it tells us 'clearly belief in the most favoured sense is so-and-so, in detail'; but that does not tell us why it is so, why it must be so, and why this must be the most favoured case. As an insight, it need not be mistaken: but we require a deduction as well as an exposition of such a concept. It is a condition of the application of the concept of belief in the non-favoured cases that we should be unhesitating in applying it to the favoured cases: but that this is a condition and a necessary one requires to be shown.

I am concerned with the question, 'What kind of concept is belief?'. That question is not the same precisely as the question, 'What is belief?' for the upshot of the investigation so far is that belief is the kind of concept which makes the question, 'What is belief?' unanswerable, at least in so far as it requests a general description which will cover all cases of belief and nothing else. But the matter cannot possibly rest there. For a concept of which this was all that can be said might be a possible concept, but never a concept which could ever be attributed to anyone. A man who said, 'I have a strange concept of something which is connected with nothing else and which I simply know when to apply as I know how to apply the concepts of pain, willing, feeling happy, etc.' could not only not simply be taken at his word, but would be in no position to take *himself* at his word: for the difficulty is not in saying whether what he says is true, but in saying *what* he is saying. And certainly, the concept of belief is not only applicable with authority to ourselves, but with confidence to others. We are able to tell, if not incorrigibly, what others believe. 'Belief' introduces a concept in the public language. For this to be possible there must be more that we can say about the nature of the concept. So far as belief is a *b*-concept and a concept of the public language, it is necessary not only that it should be applicable as a *b*-concept, incorrigibly, to oneself, but also it must be applicable outside the first person, and such application will require justification in terms of conditions which are expressible only in the third person, and hence require application of *a*-concepts. The problem of other minds is largely the problem of how *b*-concepts are capable of use in this way, as if they were *a*-concepts. How, in particular, this is possible in the case of the concept of belief is our problem. For in order that it should be possible, there must be some kind of *necessary* connexions, and not merely contingent ones, with *a*-concepts. That is, the concept of belief as one in the public language could not be applied at all, unless there were in general conditions coming under *a*-concepts which were able to justify its application to others. The connexion between belief and such conditions—between belief and observable assertion and action, for example—is not like the connexion between belief and the pulse-rate, so that lying makes one's heart beat faster. They are not, like that, discovered (and we thus dispose of all simple arguments from analogy in dealing with the problem of other minds), but connexions which must be presupposed for any such discoveries to be possible. There must be general conditions which count as evidence (which however may be overridden by first person testimony) for its correct application to others. But what we have so far observed seems to make this question unanswerable: belief is not explicable in terms of other concepts, such as assertion, action or evidence: so how can there be any necessary connexions between these and belief?

That is my problem, and what follows I hope is some kind of answer.

There is one further way in which a connexion may be made between belief on the one hand and evidence, assertion and action on the other. It is this. Belief, we have seen, is somehow connected with truth: for the mode of consciousness called belief is distinguishable from other modes of consciousness only in terms of modes of language, in terms of statements rather than commands or questions. But of course what is believed is not thereby true; it is only thereby something which is either true or false. But it is *wrong* to believe what is false, and *right* to believe what is true. Whatever else one does with a truth, believing the proposition that expresses it is the first and most fitting thing to do with it—before we start deploring it or trying to alter it, for example. The connexion between belief and truth is that belief is *appropriate* to truth; it is proper only when it is of what is true, and only intelligible, therefore, when it is of what *could* be true.[1]

To say this is not to say *what* belief is, nor is it to establish any necessary connexion between belief and any *actual* condition. It establishes a connexion which does not necessarily, but which *ought* to hold; it is what we demand of belief, whether or not we expect it. But that what is true ought to be believed is not something which we have discovered to be so, that might have been otherwise, as we might discover that roses ought to be pruned. Because demanding this of belief is the only condition which makes it a possible concept of the public language. To say, 'Belief is appropriate to truth' is to answer the question, 'How is belief identified as a public concept? How are we able to pick out belief and talk about it in common?'

It is only this tenuous connexion which reaches out from the unanalysable private state of mind to the public world. It is enough, however, to explain the connexions with evidence, assertion, etc., which puzzled us. The connexion with assertion is that belief is the appropriate attitude to truth and the inappropriate attitude to falsity. It is a mode of consciousness, therefore, that can be picked out only in terms of that which may be true or false, in terms of assertions rather than commands or exclamations. The connexion with evidence is a consequence of this. The conditions of the appropriateness of the assertion of truth (where the truth, as opposed to the politeness or the relevance of a remark is in question) must themselves be conditions of the appropriateness of belief; for what is appropriate in a given situation is appropriate when that situation is demanded by some further conditions. Again, if it is appropriate to believe p only when p, and if it is appropriate to do x when p, then it is appropriate to do x when believing p. This explains the connexion between belief and action, and also the direction we normally think this dependence takes: action waits on belief, and belief waits on evidence.

[1] Cf. Willing is the attitude which is appropriate to actions which are right: it is only proper when it is of what is right, and only intelligible therefore when it is of what could be right—that is, actions.

This also explains the necessity for those paradigm cases which Findlay takes to constitute the most favoured cases of belief. If these cases of belief were not belief at all, then we are not counting as belief the attitude of mind which we would expect to be present when the truth is most compellingly manifest, when the conditions for the assertion of truth are best satisfied. It would be possible, I suppose, for Tertullian to bring up children so that they said 'I believe' not only of the ridiculous things he believed, but of and only of every ridiculous thing. But what would they be saying of themselves when they said they believed? There would be no possible ground in this case for saying that they were using the word 'belief' in our sense at all: that whatever, if anything, they were saying of themselves, we could not identify it with that which we say when *we* say 'I believe' of ourselves. People brought up to speak in this way would deny that they believe in cases where the appropriateness of the assertion of truth is most clearly exhibited to them as well as to us; and they would insist they believe in those cases where by their own and our standards the assertion of truth is least appropriate. It would be most plausible to say that what they meant by 'I believe *p*' is 'I think *p* is ridiculous'. If they denied this, however (and we could somehow take at its face value the assertion of the denial) we should not know what to say: are their standards of appropriateness of the assertion of truth different from ours? And if so what are they standards of—are they standards of truth any more? To say such things makes it impossible for us to say not only that they accept the standards of appropriateness that we accept, but what it is they are accepting or thinking. We certainly have no right to speak of belief in their case. The acceptance of such standards of appropriateness, then, by others, is a necessary condition of the propriety of our attributing the concept of belief—let alone belief itself—to them. And the existence of the paradigm cases is all that allows us to say that they do accept such standards. (Of course, it is equally much a condition of our applying these concepts to ourselves: but there would not be much sense in doubting whether or not we ourselves accept such standards.)

I should make it clear that I am not arguing that belief *becomes* a concept of the public language by our demanding that it shall be of what is true. I do not want to say: there is first the concept of belief which is the concept of a purely private object, and this concept becomes public by the demand that we make that what is true shall be believed and what is false shall not. A purely private concept would have to be one which had no possible application beyond the first person, that is, one whose application was never dependent on conditions which come under *a*-concepts. But if so it is difficult to see how any purely private concept could *ever* become public: for its connexion with public conditions would be in *every* case contingent: so that taking any public condition as evidence of the correctness of its application would always be a pure assumption no better than any other. These difficulties are additional to the prior one that is involved in speaking of the possibility of a private language, that is, of the possibility of the application in general of any private concepts whatsoever.

What I am arguing is that the concept of belief is only possible *at all*—since it is a concept in the public language—if we presuppose standards of appropriateness which link belief with what is believed. It follows that any qualitative characteristics that one may associate with belief cannot be essential for its identification; it is for this reason that we cannot say that belief is necessarily a feeling. On the other hand it is a mode of consciousness. Though not essentially marked by a difference of quality, it is not merely nothing for us.

I have said that belief is one mode of consciousness where *will* is another. It should be possible to say similar things about will. The first-person statements 'I intend', 'I mean to', etc., are in an important range of cases incorrigible, and apparent counter-examples may be dealt with in a similar way to those encountered in discussing belief. Attempts to explain willing as an *a*-concept—to reduce it to a tendency to act for example—would be on the same kind of shoals as attempts to explain belief as an *a*-concept. It would either involve circularity or misrepresent the concept of will as always corrigible in its first-person application. Will cannot be reduced to any set of *b*-concepts; but it can be picked out only in relation to commands, expressions of intentions, etc.; it consists in thinking these seriously. But how can we distinguish thinking them seriously from merely entertaining them? What is the difference between intending to do something and merely dwelling on the idea of it? I should argue that will or intention is what we demand of possible actions that are right, as belief is what we demand of possible propositions that are true. This means that the concept of intention or will would be impossible unless in general we regarded it as appropriate to do what is right, that is unless we were able to distinguish actions according to some criteria which allowed us to speak of reasons for doing one thing rather than another.

If this is so, then people can be spoken of as acting with intention, or as willing, in general, only so far as they are conceived as thinking things right. But it may also be argued[1] that the concept of what it is right to do or what there are reasons for doing is applicable to people only in so far as they in general tend to do what they believe is right (divergences requiring special explanation). That there can be said to be such a thing as will or intention (i.e., that the concept of will or intention can ever be applied) requires publicly intelligible standards of correct behaviour and an actual tendency to follow them: something like a human nature, so to speak. Similarly, one can speak of people as believing only so far as they can be conceived as thinking things true, and as accepting criteria which enable them to distinguish the false from the true. But one could speak of people as accepting these criteria of truth only in so far as in general they are willing to assert (that is, do assert unless there are some special reasons for not doing so) what these criteria demand, on occasions when assertion is in place. And this means that there could not be said to be such a thing as belief, unless there were publicly intelligible standards of evidence and an actual tendency to use them: something like common sense, so to speak.

[1] As I did in 'Acting with Reason', *Philosophical Quarterly*, No. 33 (1958).

X

IS JUSTIFIED TRUE BELIEF KNOWLEDGE?

EDMUND L. GETTIER

VARIOUS attempts have been made in recent years to state necessary and sufficient conditions for someone's knowing a given proposition. The attempts have often been such that they can be stated in a form similar to the following:[1]

(a) S knows that P *IFF* (i) P is true,
(ii) S believes that P, and
(iii) S is justified in believing that P.

For example, Chisholm has held that the following gives the necessary and sufficient conditions for knowledge:[2]

(b) S knows that P *IFF* (i) S accepts P,
(ii) S has adequate evidence for P, and
(iii) P is true.

Ayer has stated the necessary and sufficient conditions for knowledge as follows:[3]

(c) S knows that P *IFF* (i) P is true,
(ii) S is sure that P is true, and
(iii) S has the right to be sure that P is true.

I shall argue that (a) is false in that the conditions stated therein do not constitute a *sufficient* condition for the truth of the proposition that S knows that P. The same argument will show that (b) and (c)

From *Analysis*, Vol. 23 (Blackwell, 1963), pp. 121–3. Reprinted by permission of the author, *Analysis*, and Basil Blackwell.

[1] Plato seems to be considering some such definition at *Theaetetus* 201, and perhaps accepting one at *Meno* 98.

[2] Roderick M. Chisholm, *Perceiving: a Philosophical Study*, Cornell University Press (Ithaca, New York, 1957), p. 16.

[3] A. J. Ayer, *The Problem of Knowledge*, Macmillan (London, 1956), p. 34.

fail if 'has adequate evidence for' or 'has the right to be sure that' is substituted for 'is justified in believing that' throughout.

I shall begin by noting two points. First, in that sense of 'justified' in which S's being justified in believing P is a necessary condition of S's knowing that P, it is possible for a person to be justified in believing a proposition that is in fact false. Secondly, for any proposition P, if S is justified in believing P, and P entails Q, and S deduces Q from P and accepts Q as a result of this deduction, then S is justified in believing Q. Keeping these two points in mind, I shall now present two cases in which the conditions stated in (a) are true for some proposition, though it is at the same time false that the person in question knows that proposition.

Case I:

Suppose that Smith and Jones have applied for a certain job. And suppose that Smith has strong evidence for the following conjunctive proposition:

(d) Jones is the man who will get the job, and Jones has ten coins in his pocket.

Smith's evidence for (d) might be that the president of the company assured him that Jones would in the end be selected, and that he, Smith, had counted the coins in Jones's pocket ten minutes ago. Proposition (d) entails:

(e) The man who will get the job has ten coins in his pocket.

Let us suppose that Smith sees the entailment from (d) to (e), and accepts (e) on the grounds of (d), for which he has strong evidence. In this case, Smith is clearly justified in believing that (e) is true.

But imagine, further, that unknown to Smith, he himself, not Jones, will get the job. And, also, unknown to Smith, he himself has ten coins in his pocket. Proposition (e) is then true, though proposition (d), from which Smith inferred (e), is false. In our example, then, all of the following are true: *(i)* (e) is true, *(ii)* Smith believes that (e) is true, and *(iii)* Smith is justified in believing that (e) is true. But it is equally clear that Smith does not *know* that (e) is true; for (e) is true in virtue of the number of coins in Smith's pocket, while Smith does not know how many coins are in Smith's pocket, and bases his belief in (e) on a count of the coins in Jones's pocket, whom he falsely believes to be the man who will get the job.

Case II:

Let us suppose that Smith has strong evidence for the following proposition:

(f) Jones owns a Ford.

Smith's evidence might be that Jones has at all times in the past within Smith's memory owned a car, and always a Ford, and that Jones has just offered Smith a ride while driving a Ford. Let us imagine, now, that Smith has another friend, Brown, of whose whereabouts he is totally ignorant. Smith selects three place-names quite at random, and constructs the following three propositions:

(g) Either Jones owns a Ford, or Brown is in Boston;
(h) Either Jones owns a Ford, or Brown is in Barcelona;
(i) Either Jones owns a Ford, or Brown is in Brest-Litovsk.

Each of these propositions is entailed by (f). Imagine that Smith realizes the entailment of each of these propositions he has constructed by (f), and proceeds to accept (g), (h), and (i) on the basis of (f). Smith has correctly inferred (g), (h), and (i) from a proposition for which he has strong evidence. Smith is therefore completely justified in believing each of these three propositions. Smith, of course, has no idea where Brown is.

But imagine now that two further conditions hold. First, Jones does *not* own a Ford, but is at present driving a rented car. And secondly, by the sheerest coincidence, and entirely unknown to Smith, the place mentioned in proposition (h) happens really to be the place where Brown is. If these two conditions hold then Smith does *not* know that (h) is true, even though *(i)* (h) *is* true, *(ii)* Smith does believe that (h) is true, and *(iii)* Smith is justified in believing that (h) is true.

These two examples show that definition (a) does not state a *sufficient* condition for someone's knowing a given proposition. The same cases, with appropriate changes, will suffice to show that neither definition (b) nor definition (c) do so either.

XI

BELIEF AND CONSTRAINT

BERNARD MAYO

I

DISCUSSIONS of belief seldom succeed in ridding themselves entirely of a conceptual model which is easily seen to be absurd yet which proves oddly resistant to eviction. Central to any discussion of belief is the question of the relation between belief and the truth. Truth is independent of belief, since anything that is believed can be false. (This is not affected by apparent exceptions where truth does depend on belief, as where the existence of a belief verifies the statement asserting this very fact, or is causally related to facts which verify other statements.) But belief is not independent of truth, and this in two ways: (1) what is believed must be either true or false (the formal object of belief is always a proposition. More strongly, a belief cannot exist without there being some form of words which would count as its expression); and (2) what is believed, even if it happens to be false, is believed *to be true*. Now on the general and, until comparatively recently, unquestioned assumption that belief is an act or state of mind, the problem of relating this act or state of mind to something that is not an act or state of mind, viz., the truth, was a formidable, and indeed insuperable, problem which only the covert use of an incoherent model was able to gloss over.

It is, to begin with, clearly necessary that any proposition which someone is to believe should be, at least at some time and in some guise, present to his consciousness: it must, as the jargon had it, be entertained. Now a dilemma appears. Either the proposition is entertained without commitment to belief in its truth—i.e., is entertained as only possibly true—or it is entertained as true. If the former, then the problem on our hands is how we advance from entertainment to belief; if the latter, this problem is merely shelved, for we still want to know what distinguishes entertaining as true—which is now

From *Proceedings of the Aristotelian Society*, Vol. 64 (1963–4), pp. 139–56. Reprinted by courtesy of the author and the Editor of the Aristotelian Society.

just a rephrasal of 'believing'—from entertaining as merely possibly true. A definition of 'belief' taken from F. C. S. Schiller nicely exemplifies this dilemma: belief, says Schiller, is definable as 'the spiritual attitude of welcome which we assume towards what we take to be a truth'.[1] If the last few words are read literally, taking something to be a truth *is* believing it, so the definition is viciously circular and the mention of 'welcome' redundant; if they are taken in any other sense, such as entertaining as possibly true, then the 'spiritual attitude of welcome' is premature and irrational, and the definition false.

Schiller also speaks of a 'natural disposition of the mind to welcome truth' which is what gives content to his definition, and we find many similar remarks in Newman's treatise: for example, 'It is the law of my mind to seal up the conclusions to which ratiocination has brought me, by that formal assent which I have called a certitude'.[2] This implies a conceptual gap between accepting something as true, in this case a proof, and assenting to it; and indeed Newman immediately goes on to concede that there can be actual exceptions to his 'law'. But it is perplexing in the extreme to try to open a gap between accepting something as true and believing it; yet a determined effort to locate a conceptual gap between belief and *something* else—a gap which certainly has to exist—results only in a tantalizing elusiveness in this other term. What, I suspect, one would secretly like to think, and what the model in fact lures us to think, is that truth can, as it were, enter half-way into our consciousness, exerting on us a mysterious influence, now minatory, now winning, to which we usually, but not always, respond with acts of assent; these acts are fully voluntary, and if we speak of being 'constrained to believe', this is only because our sympathies are so fully engaged. We should perhaps like to think something like this, but we should do so at a heavy cost in intellectual honesty.

Newman, as this remark suggests, is very much an heir to the traditional empiricist philosophy of mind. Consider, for example, how his doctrine of real and notional assent is a direct descendant, and refinement, of Hume's doctrine of belief in terms of degrees of vivacity. It might be thought that it was the prevailing commitment to this ultra-empiricist philosophy of mind that generated the difficulties about belief. Actually, in the passage immediately following, Newman makes it clear that he is not thinking of an empirical law connecting belief with whatever is before the mind, so

[1] *Problems of Belief*, p. 14.

[2] *Grammar of Assent*, vii.2.2.

much as a normative law: he goes on, 'I could indeed have withheld my assent' (for assent is always voluntary), 'but I should have acted against my nature, had I done so when there was what I considered a proof; and I did only what was fitting, what was incumbent upon me, upon those conditions, in giving it'. Compare this remark, with its mention of what is 'fitting' and 'incumbent', with some remarks of a modern philosopher who certainly cannot be accused of subscribing to the traditional philosophy of mind (though I shall argue that he has not sufficiently disengaged himself from it): Mr. A. P. Griffiths in his recent, very challenging, paper 'On Belief', delivered to this Society last year: they form a key passage on which his thesis rests:

> 'It is *wrong* to believe what is false, and *right* to believe what is true. Whatever else one does with a truth, believing the proposition which expresses it is the first and most fitting thing to do with it—before we start deploring it or trying to alter it, for example' (p. 182).[1]

This is excellent counter-propaganda to Marx's epitaph, but it is also just as incoherent, just as symptomatic of an unworkable conceptual model, as our other examples. This truth that we are going to do something with: do we, or do we not, recognize it for what it is? If we do, we already believe it; if we do not, we cannot start to deplore, or try to alter, *it*, but only something else, whatever we mistake *it* for. How could we deplore or try to change what we do not believe to be the case? But talk of what we ought to do, of what is fitting, is out of place if we cannot choose but do—or not do—whatever it may be.

(Notice that these difficulties about belief and the truth are closely paralleled by the paradoxes about the good discussed by Plato in *Meno* 77–8. Not everything that men pursue is good; not everything that men believe is true. But everything that men pursue is pursued *sub specie boni*; and everything that men believe is believed *sub specie veri*.)

I believe that in giving a central place in his analysis to the notion of a norm, standard, or criterion, Griffiths has got something very important and enlightening; but he has got it by the wrong end of the stick. To over-simplify very considerably, he should not say 'It is wrong to believe what is false'; he should say 'What is false is what it is wrong to believe'. I hope to elaborate and substantiate this.

II

For Griffiths, the central problem about belief is just a particular

[1] [Pages 139–140 of this volume. Ed.]

case of the other-minds problem-nexus. A crude formulation of the problem, which Griffiths would disavow, is: We know what our own beliefs are; how do we know that, and what, others believe? Griffiths does not deny that we have 'privileged access' to our own beliefs, on the contrary he affirms that we do, but he insists that the concept of belief, being a concept of the public language (or, being a concept *tout court*, if we eschew the notion of a private language) must be rooted in the conditions of its ascription to people in general.

We are to distinguish, among concepts, what I will call *O*-concepts and *P*-concepts (not here following Griffiths' terminology or, for that matter, Strawson's). The difference between them turns on the conditions warranting their ascription to people; *P*-concepts being those for the ascription of which to a given person, that person himself is in a specially authoritative position, in that only he can say with finality (though he need not choose to say with truth) that the concept in question applies to him; in other words, it makes sense to ask whether a person, in ascribing an *O*-predicate, either to himself or to someone else, might be making a mistake, but it does not make sense to ask whether a person, in ascribing a *P*-predicate to himself, could be making a mistake, though in applying it to someone else, or to himself at a time other than the time of ascription, he may. Thus I can ask whether you are mistaken in thinking that I, you or anyone else is feverish, blushing, etc., or whether you are mistaken in thinking that I or he is in pain, embarrassed, or believes that swans can fly, but *not* whether you are mistaken in thinking that you are in pain, embarrassed, or believe that swans can fly.

How can anyone ever know that the conditions requisite for the application of a *P*-concept are ever satisfied? Or as Griffiths puts it, how can a *P*-word ever become part of the public language? The difficulty as he sees it is that no set of criteria of a given type will determine the applicability of the belief-concept, for, to mention the familiar difficulties, what a person says may be insincere; behaviour conditions notoriously fail, both because behaviour is a clue to belief only in the light of assumed wants and aversions (themselves *P*-concepts), and because it is in any case not *behaviour*, but *action*, that is correlated with belief and wanting, and action is a *P*-concept since it involves knowing what one is doing; finally, even if we admitted feelings, the feelings that attend belief are far too varied to constitute belief.

The only point at which the *P*-concept of *belief* can be anchored in the public language, according to Griffiths, is the notion of truth.

But since one may believe what is not true, and what is true may not be believed, this has to be modified immediately to the form: belief is what is *appropriate* to truth. 'The first and foremost thing to do with a truth is to believe it.' It is, I think, because a norm, standard or criterion of the proper covers the possible as well as the actual, indeed concerns the possible instead of the actual, that Griffiths thinks it a necessary step in the admission-procedure of *P*-concepts to the public language.

Griffiths himself notes in his paper that what he says about belief can also be said about willing. Just as belief is appropriate to what is true, so willing is appropriate to what is right. If 'willing' is either a typical member of, or an omnibus-word for, the family of concepts trying, deciding to, intending, setting about, etc., one presumes that the parallel with belief also extends backwards to an identical initial problem about criteria of ascription: we cannot determine what a person actually intends either from what he says, or from what he does, or even from feelings however fully and veraciously reported, since it is never self-contradictory to say that a person announces certain intentions, performs certain actions, or (or even and) undergoes certain emotions, and yet actually does not have the intention which putatively he has. One can only say, then, that such an intention, whether he actually has it or not, is what is 'appropriate' to a certain publicly characterizable situation, namely where some act is morally (or perhaps otherwise) incumbent on him.

III

An immediate consequence of the thesis that believing is what it is fitting to do with a truth is, of course, that one ought (not necessarily in the moral sense) to believe what is true and disbelieve what is false. Further, one ought never to suspend judgement, since there is nothing that it is right *not* to believe, except the false, the negation of which, being true, one ought to believe. And if *ought* implies both *can* and its subcontrary *can omit*, it follows that believing is something we can do or avoid, an act we can perform or a state we can enter into, or depart from, at will. And it is no use saying that *ought* implies *can* and its subcontrary only in its moral field of operation; if the implication holds at all, it holds universally, not only in other fields of operation but even in secondary, tertiary and degenerate senses of 'ought': if there ought to be an eclipse next year, then there can be one, and there can be none.

This consequence, that belief is voluntary, is contrary to common sense and much ordinary language and has been generally disfavoured by philosophers; it was defended, notoriously, by Descartes and William James, and also, incidentally, by Newman and Schiller, and roundly rejected in more recent writings such as those of Price,[1] Grant[2] and Evans.[3] There certainly are conflicting prima facie considerations. In favour of voluntarism is the fact that we assume responsibility for our beliefs, sometimes having reached them after protracted and perhaps agonizing deliberation, speaking of commitment and decision and generally placing them at the farthest possible remove from things like falling downstairs. ('I happen to believe . . .' is strictly ironical.) On the other hand we speak of being constrained to believe . . . or forced to conclude . . . or being unable to resist the weight of evidence . . . and generally using the well-worn mechanical metaphors that suggest that belief is, after all, something that happens like falling downstairs; a contradiction which is enhanced by the consideration that *any* attempt to assert freedom of action here, to believe what one chooses, is irrational, and the more rational a man is, the less freedom he has to decide what he will believe.

The only way of escaping this dilemma is, of course, to reinterpret the mechanical metaphors of constraint, force and so on. An interpretation which is altogether too facile is to treat them all as cases of logical compulsion. Someone who accepts the premises and validity of an argument will also accept the conclusion; if we choose to say that he 'must' accept it, we only mean that if he does not, he is inconsistent, irrational, etc. So the man himself may say that he is 'forced' to accept the conclusion, meaning only that if he does not he will be irrational. Similarly it might be argued that a man who is constrained to perform some moral duty is just a man who knows that if he does not do it, he will be acting immorally. But this is far too drastic an emasculation of the 'force' metaphors. In both cases, it ignores the fact that, very often, a man has no choice but to be rational, or to be moral, and what sort of restriction is this?

A somewhat more promising explanation of the 'force' metaphors, and a possible defence of the view that belief is subject to will, is to compare a specific case of belief with a specific case of moral duty.

The clearest cases of belief being apparently *not* subject to will

[1] H. H. Price, 'Belief and Will', *P. A. S., Suppl. Vol.* 28 (1954).

[2] C. K. Grant, 'Belief and Action', *Inaugural Lecture*, University of Durham (1960).

[3] J. L. Evans, 'Error and the Will', *Philosophy* 38 (1963), p. 136.

are those in which the evidence is so overwhelmingly strong that a person who could fail to believe, in face of the evidence, would have to be completely deranged. But if he were, then *ex hypothesi* he would not be in control of his belief; whereas if he were not, then again he could not help believing what he does believe. But, so the present explanation goes, there are also cases of actions which, though physically within my power, I am in the same way utterly incapable of perpetrating or withholding; where it is the moral obligation that is so overwhelmingly stringent that a person who could act despite it would be beyond the pale of responsibility. Then, *ex hypothesi*, he would not be in control of his actions; but if he is a normal responsible person, then again he cannot help acting as he does. Yet this does not prove that his act is not such as we can properly describe as 'what he ought to do'. No more, then, does the fact that someone cannot help believing what the evidence overwhelmingly testifies to, prove that the proposition in question is not one that we can properly describe as 'what he ought to believe'.

However, this argument is an *ignoratio elenchi*. For what corresponds to belief, in terms of the original thesis, is not an *action* but an 'act' of will, an intention or decision. What a person ought to *do* does not involve a *P*-concept; what does, or rather what is, is the concept applicable to a person who intends or is setting himself to do what he ought. Now it is true that we often do indulge in or accept not only exhortations to do what is right, but also exhortations to do so 'in the right frame of mind', 'from a sense of duty', 'because we ought', 'for the right reason' and so forth. This supports, thus far, Griffiths' view that there are states of mind appropriate to what is right; it seems that two sets of criteria are at work, one to determine what is right (which correspond to truth-criteria), and the other to determine what a person ought to feel in relation to what is right (which correspond to the criteria postulated by the normative theory of belief). And the question, whether we can choose to believe, is paralleled, not by the question, whether we can choose to act, but by the question, whether we can choose to feel, intend, etc. Which is indeed the same question, the answer to which appears to be, No. We can exhort someone to act—which implies that he can choose to act or not to act—and we can also perhaps exhort him to act in a certain frame of mind, but we cannot mean to imply that it is up to him which frame of mind he chooses to do it in, which of a range of feelings he chooses to select as that of which his action shall be the outcome. Whatever analysis we are to give of the admittedly prevalent tokens of admiration or disapproval of the states of mind in which, motives from which, people do what they ought to do, it is not this.

IV

I have already said enough about the queerness of any dictum to the effect that believing is what we ought to do with a truth. I now want to note that the general thesis of which this dictum is a consequence—the thesis that a *P*-concept, at least in the cases of believing and willing, can admit of public conditions of applicability only under the aegis of a normative rubric—fails in any case to do the job required of it; unless, that is, the norms in question are looked for at quite a different place. Belief is what is fitting to truth. This does not tell us *what* belief is, Griffiths says, but how belief is publicly identified. *What* belief is can only be characterized as an 'unanalysable private state of mind', 'a mode of consciousness', something that is 'not nothing for us'—enigmatic remarks which reveal the ghost of the psychological empiricism that he has not quite exorcized—but it is publicly identified as whatever satisfies the normative rubric. But we may well ask whether anything *can* be identified purely as whatever satisfies a rule, norm or criterion of appropriateness. Does not the very meaning of 'rule', 'criterion', etc., evaporate if there is no way of independently identifying states of affairs which are to count as satisfying or not satisfying the rule? The only remotely plausible sort of analogical example I can think of is one which ultimately tells against Griffiths' analysis and in favour of mine. At first it might seem that what Griffiths says about the concept *belief* could be said about the concept *wife*: what a wife is, the person she is, is quite independent of any rules of wifely status, but the concept *wife* is a concept of the public language, and a particular person is identified as a wife, solely in virtue of certain normative rubrics, legal in force, such as that a wife is whoever it is other than whom one ought not to cohabit with . . .; just so, allegedly, a belief is whatever state of mind one ought not to have in regard to a falsehood. But this analogy is obviously bogus. The true parallel to the latter statement is: 'Cohabitation is what one ought not to do with a non-wife', and the true parallel to the former is 'A truth is any proposition other than those one ought not to believe'. The norm-backed concept *wife* is explicated *via* a non-normative concept perfectly applicable without the norm; similarly, I think, *truth* is a norm-backed concept explicable *via* a non-normative concept *belief* which is already applicable independently of the norm.

V

I locate the initial mistake of the normative theory of belief at the point where it was said that a normative rubric is required to take care of the extension of *P*-concepts to the possible as well as, or rather instead of, the actual. (Belief is not believing something that *is* true, but believing something *as* true.) Now why should it be thought that only gerundive generalizations can cover the possible? Why not indicative generalizations? Any general statement, just as much as any rule, and just in virtue of its being general, must necessarily extend to the possible. Why should we not say, instead of

1. Belief is what is appropriate to truth
2. Willing is what is appropriate to what is right
3. Fear is what is appropriate to fearful circumstances, symptoms of fear and efforts to escape[1]
4. Pain is what is appropriate to injury

the following

1. Belief is what 'goes with' truth
2. Willing is what 'goes with' what is right
3. Fear is what 'goes with' fearful circumstances, symptoms of fear and efforts to escape
4. Pain is what 'goes with' crying?

'Goes with' is so far a deliberately vague expression, intended to convey the notion of a conceptual connexion which rests on something more than empirical correlation. A purely empirical correlation is false to the fact that people fail to believe what is true, and believe what is not true, far too frequently to count as mere exceptions to a generalization; a normative connexion has faults of its own which I have already examined; and both types of connexion, by leaving the element of truth unanalysed, fall foul of the vicious dilemma of Sec. I. A connexion between belief and something else can only be a connexion between belief and something present to the believer's mind (this is true even of the normative theory, for although it may sometimes be true that a person ought to believe something that he has never considered, it is often false that a person ought to believe something which, though it happens to be true, yet he actually has

[1] Kenny, *Action, Emotion and Will*, p. 67. Circularity is only apparent.

convincing evidence against). But attempts to characterize this connexion in the terms stated (viz., as between a belief and a proposition present to the believer), such as the state of 'entertaining', led to the paradox. The alternative is to abandon the notion of 'entertaining' and to fall back on the notion of *asserting*. Both belief and truth are conceptually—and normatively—tied to asserting.

It might be objected that we cannot give meaning to the expression '*A* asserts proposition *p*' without covertly reintroducing the notion of belief, since there are sincere and insincere assertions, insincere assertions are those which are not sincere, and sincere ones are those that are believed. I think, however, that this would be a mistake, and that the notion of assertion is conceptually prior, not posterior, to that of belief. An assertion is a speech-act performed in a standard speech-situation, where the 'standard' situation is not defined in terms of the absence of non-standard-making features.

Such standard situations are governed by rules; the speech-acts that are assertions carry information in so far as the rules are observed, misinformation in so far as they are broken: but they convey information, and misinformation, only in so far as the rules are presumed (by the listeners) *not* to have been broken: without this presumption, neither information nor misinformation is possible. But it is very important to be clear that these rules of truth-telling, so to speak, have nothing to do with moral rules about sincerity and lying, and nothing to do, as yet, with belief. They are rules which prescribe what we should say—or, rather, forbid what we should not say, on pain of saying what is false. But for those for whom this is not a pain, there are other rules which prescribe truth-telling—or, rather, again, (since the fact that some proposition is true is never, by itself, sufficient reason for saying that anyone ought to assert it) rules which forbid saying what is false (since the fact that some proposition is false *is*, by itself, a sufficient reason for saying that no one ought to assert it). This second class of rules is, of course, the class of moral rules concerned with sincerity and deception. And the 'pain' in question—that on pain of which we are forbidden to say whatever is false—is, of course, the pain of doing what is morally wrong.

We can now introduce the concept of belief. A person who disbelieves what he says, or believes something inconsistent with what he says, is a person who is consciously[1] doing something wrong, to wit, deceiving. This divergence from the moral norm is insincerity, as distinct from the

[1] Excluding cases of self-deception, if such there be.

divergence from the rules of the indicative language-game, which was falsity. Sincerity is non-divergence from the norm; as with truth, it is the negative word that, in Austin's phrase, 'wears the trousers'.

Now it is widely held that belief, at least in very many and most typical cases, is dispositional. If belief were a disposition to say, we could evade the difficulties in the thesis that 'belief is what is appropriate to truth' thus. Either at the level of the rules of the language-game, or at the level of the moral rules, the belief-requirement is none other than the assertion-requirement, *plus*: exactly the same factor that has to be added to the action requirement of a moral rule, to wit, the so-called motive-requirement. It is not enough, morally speaking, simply to do whatever is required: it must be done 'in the right spirit', 'for the right reason', the act must spring from a natural or second-nature tendency to do that kind of act in that kind of situation. If we call this 'willing', what I have just said is a way of putting Griffiths' dictum that 'willing' is what is appropriate to what is right. In the case of assertion, the extra factor is belief—or would be, *if* belief were a disposition to say. One is required, at the language-game level, not just to say what conforms to the rules on this or that occasion, but to make a practice of doing so—on pain of not playing that particular game. And one is required, at the moral level, to make a practice of playing that particular game at all times—on pain of being a liar.

Belief is not, or at least not only, a disposition to say. But whatever else it is, it is only in so far as it *is* a disposition to say, that it is normatively tied to truth, and for the simple reason that the truth is what we are required to tell—*and* believe. Similarly intentions and motives are not, or at least not only, dispositions to act; but whatever else they are, it is only in so far as they are dispositions to act that 'willing' is normatively tied to what is right, and for the simple reason that the right (or obligatory) is what we are required to do—*and* to be disposed to do.

As for pain and fear: if it is right to say that pain is 'appropriate' to injury, yet there is no sense in speaking of a person's being required to be in pain—as there is good sense in speaking of one's being required to believe, or to intend. There is an obvious contrast between the two sets of *P*-predicates, or between 1-2, and 3-4, of the table on page 155. So it seems that the word 'appropriate' is doing an entirely different job, in the case of pain and fear, and in the case of belief and will. I think, too, that the job it is doing in the case of pain and fear is precisely the job it is *also* doing in the case of those aspects of belief, and of will, which are *not* the disposition to say, and to act, respectively. To these I now turn.

These aspects of belief are those which are often dismissed as inadequate criteria for the assignation of this *P*-predicate to other persons: (*a*) what a person says; (*b*) his behaviour being such as would in fact be conducive to his presumed goals if *p* were true; (*c*) his feelings of conviction, warm glows of assent, etc. Griffiths seems to have concluded that, since no one of these is a sufficient condition for the presence of belief, no set of them is either, so that we can only say that belief is 'not nothing' and resign ourselves to a schematic categorization in terms of what is appropriate. But I see no reason why we should not regard (*a*) to (*c*), either singly or in conjunction, as criteria—though never logically sufficient criteria—for the assignation of the belief concept; since there is a high correlation, not merely inductive, both among them, and between them and the dispositional core of belief. In other words, belief is what usually goes with assertion, or with acting in a certain manner easily interpretable in the light of usual goals, or even with certain feelings, etc. This 'goes with' can be, and perhaps is, in the case of belief and will, both indicative and gerundive; but it is only the indicative sense that is required (*a*) to give the criteria for the assignation of these *P*-predicates, and (*b*) to extend a parallel treatment to other *P*-predicates.

VI

Can it ever be right to say that someone ought to believe, disbelieve, or suspend judgement? This is obviously a complex question, which will have to be asked separately of each of the various possible components of belief. Clearly saying is doing something, and may therefore be doing something that one ought, or ought not, to do. Again, the acting envisaged in the acting-as-if theory is doing something that one perhaps ought or ought not to be doing. Feelings of warmth or overwhelming conviction, on the other hand, seem not to be the sort of thing which we can be exhorted or forbidden to have. A disposition, like a character-trait, may or may not be something that we ought or ought not to have.

If there is something that I ought to do here and now, then it is necessary, according to the universalisability thesis, that I recognize that I ought to do a similar thing on any similar occasion. It is also necessary that I recognize that anyone else, similarly placed, ought to do such a thing. Now if saying is a kind of doing, then the same will be true of saying, that is, on the assumption, at least, that we are concerned with what it is morally right to say or not to say. But this assumption is not necessary; the universalisability thesis still holds of saying, at the lower language-game level. If there is something I ought not to say now, simply because it happens to be false, then on any other occasion on which such a statement would be false, I ought not to make it; neither should anyone else.

Now a person who has recognized that there is something he ought to do, not only here and now, but on an indefinite number of possible occasions, may be described either as a person who has adopted a certain principle, or as a person who has a certain character-trait or virtuous disposition. There are many differences here, of course, one being that a person may not be conscious of his own virtues but can scarcely be unconscious (in the same sense) of the principles he has adopted: but the only difference that I want to note is that a principle more or less explicitly recognizes its own applicability to certain standard and forseeable types of situation, whereas a character-trait may exemplify itself in an indefinitely large and unforseeable variety of possible situations. Now for obvious reasons we do not adopt principles of truth-telling (as distinct from *the* principle of Truth-Telling): we could, but do not, formulate principles such as 'Whenever there is a horse in the garden, I shall say that there is a horse in the garden'. Instead, we are expected to acquire dispositions to say, or not to say, those things which, on particular occasions, we ought or ought not to say. These are beliefs. The question is, to what extent are we capable of exercising control over these dispositions?

Can we say both (i) 'I ought to do *X*' and (ii) 'I ought to adopt the principle of doing *X* whenever . . .'? But (ii) is redundant, since (i) already implies it. Can we, next, say both (i) and (iii) 'I ought to acquire a virtuous disposition towards doing *X*-like things'? Certainly (iii) is not redundant, and although there are difficulties in the view that I can intentionally change my character, they are surely not insuperable. But now consider (i′) 'I ought to say *S*'. This already involves (ii) 'I ought to adopt the principle of saying *S* whenever . . . '. But what about (iii′) 'I ought to acquire a disposition to say *S* whenever . . .'? This should be at least part of the meaning of (iv′) 'I ought to believe *p*', the only part, moreover—except for the mere uttering—which could be open to my control. But the difficulty here does not seem to be the difficulty—which I have in any case discounted—about changing my character. Beliefs are not reckoned as part of one's character. The difficulty is that (iv′) 'I ought to believe *p*' is something that I can never sincerely assert, unless I already do believe *p*. This makes it quite different from (iv) 'I ought to be generous, tolerant, etc.': for I can perfectly well be aware of the value of certain character-traits which I happen not to have, as well as the availability of certain exercises which might help me to acquire them. Yet in the case of belief, although I do know what sort of exercises help one to acquire or part with beliefs—attending to the evidence, for example—can I possibly be aware of the value of beliefs which I lack, or the faultiness of beliefs which I have?

'Ought to be doing *X*' is always compatible with 'is not doing *X*'—this follows from the principle that *ought* implies *can omit*. 'He ought to believe *p*' probably is compatible, though certainly not straightforwardly, with 'He does not believe *p*'. But 'I ought to believe *p*' is straightforwardly incompatible with 'I do not believe *p*'.

Though belief may properly be said to be required of us, it is a requirement which we ourselves cannot endorse—until after we have complied with it, if we do. In this respect belief is, after all, more comparable with a moral principle than with a character-trait. We cannot endorse the requirement that we embrace, or abandon, a moral principle—until after we have complied with it, if we do.

VII

'One can mistrust one's own senses, but not one's own belief' (Wittgenstein, *Ph. Inv.* II x). This is not because one cannot help trusting one's beliefs, but because it makes no sense to speak of trusting or mistrusting one's beliefs, though it makes perfectly good sense to speak of trusting or mistrusting those of other people. Why is this? Wittgenstein's imaginary interlocutor wanted to say, 'Surely "I believed" must tell of just the same thing in the past as "I believe" in the present'—and, we may add, 'Surely "He believes" tells of just the same thing as regards him, as "I believe" tells as regards me'. Perhaps, Wittgenstein suggests, the difference is that when I say 'I believe' I am not only describing my state of mind (as I should be describing his, if I said 'He believes') but I am also indirectly asserting the fact believed. '—As in certain circumstances I describe a photograph in order to describe the thing it is a photograph of. But then I must also be able to say that the photograph is a good one. So here too: "I believe it's raining and my belief is reliable, so it probably is raining".' But this does not make sense, if only because its correlatives do not: 'I believe it's raining and my belief is unreliable, so it may not be raining' and 'I believe it's raining and my belief is reliably untrue so it probably isn't raining'. Yet all three make perfectly good sense if 'he' and 'his' are substituted for 'I' and 'my'.

Wittgenstein's answer is the by now familiar one: that belief is a disposition of the believing person, a disposition which is shown by a person's behaviour, and by his words, including under the latter both the simple assertion of the fact believed, and the expression 'I believe'. My way of looking at the matter, however, is from the point of view of the word 'good' which occurred in the photograph analogy. The reason why I cannot trust or mistrust my own beliefs is that having a belief is not having something which favourably disposes me towards something else—the fact believed—but rather, to have a belief *is* to be favourably disposed towards something else: to asserting (or accepting) the proposition believed. If we bring the value-term 'good' out into the open with an example from the context of moral judgement, we find an exact parallel and paradigm for the belief case:

(1) He approves of capital punishment and his moral judgement is reliable, so capital punishment is probably right

(2) He approves of capital punishment and his moral judgement is unreliable, so capital punishment may be wrong

(3) He approves of capital punishment and his moral judgement is reliably perverse, so capital punishment is probably wrong

all make perfectly good sense, and epitomize the rationale of those who seek advice on moral matters. Yet the substitution of 'I' and 'my' for 'he' and 'his' produces nonsense. The substitute for (2) would be a case of expressing moral disapproval and in the same breath disavowing it; the substitute for (3) would be a case of expressing both approval and a positive readiness to disapprove. Both would be performatively self-defeating. To adapt my remark about belief: the reason why I cannot trust or mistrust my own moral principles (conscience) is that having a moral principle is not having something which favourably disposes me towards something else—the action-policy in question—but, rather, to have a moral principle is to be favourably disposed towards something else.

To conclude. In traditional terms, the theory of belief does indeed belong to the theory of value. But the paradigm evaluative expression is not '. . . *ought* to believe *p*' but '*I believe p*'.

NOTES ON THE CONTRIBUTORS

J. Cook Wilson, who died in 1915, was for many years Wykeham Professor of Logic at Oxford. His major writings were collected posthumously in two volumes under the title *Statement and Inference* (1926).

R. B. Braithwaite was Knightbridge Professor of Moral Philosophy at Cambridge from 1953 until his retirement in 1967. His book *Scientific Explanation* was published in 1953, and he has contributed many articles to philosophical periodicals.

H. H. Price was Wykeham Professor of Logic at Oxford from 1935 to 1959. Among his publications are *Perception* (1932), and *Thinking and Experience* (1953).

H. A. Prichard, who died in 1947, was White's Professor of Moral Philosophy at Oxford from 1928 to 1937. His major writings were collected by Sir David Ross in the two volumes *Moral Obligation* (1949) and *Knowledge and Perception* (1950).

Norman Malcolm is Professor of Philosophy at Cornell University. His books *Knowledge and Certainty* and *Dreaming* appeared in 1963 and 1964, and his valuable memoir *Ludwig Wittgenstein* was published in 1958.

A. D. Woozley was Professor of Philosophy at St. Andrews from 1954 to 1967, and is now a Professor at the University of Virginia. His book *The Theory of Knowledge* was published in 1949, and he produced in 1964 a valuable edition of Locke's *Essay concerning Human Understanding*.

Alan R. White has been Ferens Professor of Philosophy in the University of Hull since 1961. Among his publications are *G. E. Moore: a Critical Exposition* (1958), and *Attention* (1964), and he is the editor of *The Philosophy of Action* in the present series.

Jonathan Harrison is Professor of Philosophy at the University of Nottingham. He has published many articles in philosophical periodicals.

A. Phillips Griffiths (the editor of the present volume) is Professor of Philosophy at the University of Warwick. He has contributed many articles to philosophical periodicals.

Edmund L. Gettier is a member of the Department of Philosophy at Wayne State University in Michigan.

Bernard Mayo is a member of the Department of Philosophy at the University of Birmingham, and a former editor of the periodical *Analysis*. His book *Ethics and the Moral Life* appeared in 1958.

BIBLIOGRAPHY

(not including material in this volume)

THE following books are essential reading for those who wish to gain a balanced view of the issues raised in this volume:

1. Ayer, A. J.: *The Problem of Knowledge* (Macmillan, London, 1956).
2. Chisholm, R. M.: *Perceiving: A Philosophical Study* (Cornell U. P., Ithaca, N. Y., 1957).

   Theory of Knowledge (Prentice-Hall: Foundations of Philosophy Series, Englewood Cliffs, N. J., 1966) (esp. Chap. 1).
3. Findlay, J. N.: *Values and Intentions* (Allen & Unwin, London, 1961).
4. Hintikka, Jaakko: *Knowledge and Belief* (Cornell U. P., Ithaca, N. Y., 1962).
5. Moore, G. E.: Some Main Problems of Philosophy (Allen & Unwin, London, 1953) (esp. Chaps. IV, XIV & XV).
6. Wittgenstein, L.: *Philosophical Investigations* (Blackwell, Oxford, 1953).

   (Remarks relevant to knowledge and to belief are to be found throughout the book, too numerous to detail here. See, for example, Part II, Remark X on belief.)
7. Woozley, A. D.: *Theory of Knowledge* (Hutchinson, London, 1949).

In addition the reader should study a most influential article omitted from this collection on the grounds of its length and the fact that it is readily available elsewhere:

8. Austin, J. L.: 'Other Minds'. Originally published in *Proceedings of the Aristotelian Society*, Supplementary Volume XX (1946); reprinted in Flew (Ed.), *Logic and Language* (Blackwell, Oxford 1953), and Austin's *Philosophical Papers* (Ed. Urmson & Warnock, Clarendon Press, Oxford, 1961).

Austin's attack on the 'descriptive fallacy' in giving an account of knowledge is discussed in Jonathan Harrison's article 'Knowing and Promising' in the present volume. Another influential article which argues that the use of 'I know' should not be regarded as describing a state of affairs is:

9. Urmson, J. O.: 'Parenthetical Verbs', *Mind*, Vol. LXI (1952), p. 480.

A trenchant criticism of the notion of the descriptive fallacy and its application to knowledge is to be found in:

10. Geach, P. T.: 'Assertion', *Philosophical Review*, Vol. LXXIV (1965), pp. 449–465.

An important issue concerned with knowledge and belief, the nature of our knowledge of our own intentions, decisions and actions has not been dealt with in this volume. The most important sources for the discussion of this issue are:

11. Anscombe, G. E. M.: *Intention* (Blackwell, Oxford, 1957).
12. Hart, H. L. A., & Hampshire, S.: 'Decision, Intention and Certainty'. *Mind*, Vol. LXVII (1958), pp. 1–12.
13. Hampshire, S.: *Thought and Action* (Chatto & Windus, London, 1959).
14. Melden, A.: *Free Action* (Routledge and Kegan Paul, London, 1961).

These issues are also discussed in:

15. Braybrooke, D. and others: 'Some Questions for Miss Anscombe about Intention', *Analysis*, Vol. 22 (1962), pp. 49–54.
16. Anscombe, G. E. M.: 'On Sensations of Position', *Analysis*, Vol. 22 (1962), pp. 55–58.
17. Donnellan, K. S.: 'Knowing What I am Doing', *Journal of Philosophy*, Vol. LX (1963), pp. 401–409.
18. Jones, O. R.: 'Things Known without Observation', *Proceedings of the Aristotelian Society*, Vol. LXI, (1960–61).
19. Thalberg, I.: 'Foreknowledge and Decision in Advance', *Analysis*, Vol. 24 (1963–4), pp. 49–53.
20. Roxbee-Cox, J. W.: 'Can I Know beforehand what I am going to Decide?', *Philosophical Review*, Vol. LXXII (1963), pp. 88–92.

A topic which is briefly considered by Mayo and Phillips Griffiths in their articles in this volume is whether belief is subject to will. This question is further discussed in:

21. Price, H. H.: 'Belief and Will', *Proceedings of the Aristotelian Society*, Supplementary Volume XXVIII (1954), pp. 1–26.
22. Evans, J. L.: 'Error and the Will', *Philosophy*, Vol. XXXVIII, (1963) pp. 136–148.
23. Hampshire, S.: *Thought and Action*, Chap. 2 (Chatto & Windus, London, 1959).

Another important topic only touched on in this volume (e.g. by Woozley) is the distinction between 'knowing how' and 'knowing that'. The reader should consult:

24. Ryle, G.: 'Knowing How and Knowing That', *Proceedings of the Aristotelian Society*, Vol. XLVI, (1945–46), pp. 1–16.
25. Ryle, G.: *The Concept of Mind* (Hutchinson, London, 1949).

This is also discussed in:
26. Hartland-Swann: 'Logical Status of "Knowing That"', *Analysis*, Vol. 16 (1955–6), pp. 11–115.
27. Ammerman, R.: 'A note on "Knowing That"', *Analysis*, Vol. 17 (1956–7), pp. 30–32.
28. Rowland, Jane: '"Knowing How" and "Knowing that"', *Philosophical Review*, Vol. LXVII, (1958).

The earlier version of the article by Professor Malcolm reprinted in this volume, which was published in *Mind* (Vol. LXI, 1952), has been discussed in:
29. Harrison, J.: 'Mr. Malcolm on "Knowledge and Belief"', *Analysis*, Vol. 13 (1952–3), pp. 66–71.
30. Taylor, R.: 'A note on Knowing and Belief', *Analysis*, Vol. 13 (1952–3), pp. 143–144.
31. Malcolm, N.: 'On Knowledge and Belief', *Analysis*, Vol. 14 (1953–4), pp. 94–98.
32. Taylor, R.: 'A Rejoinder to Mr. Malcolm', *Analysis*, Vol. 14 (1953–4), pp. 98–99.

Gettier's article, reprinted in this volume, has been discussed in:
33. Clark, Michael: 'Knowledge and Grounds: A comment on Mr. Gettier's Paper', *Analysis*, Vol. 24, (1953–4), pp. 46–48.
34. Lehrer, K.: 'Knowledge, Truth, and Evidence', *Analysis*, Vol. 25 (1964–5), pp. 168–175.
35. Sosa, E.: 'The Analysis of "Knowledge that *p*"', *Analysis*, Vol. 25 1964–5), pp. 1–8.
36. Saunders, J. T. and Champawat, N.: 'Mr. Clark's Definition of "Knowledge"', *Analysis*, Vol. 25 (1964–5), pp. 8–9.
37. Chisholm, R.: *Theory of Knowledge* (Prentice-Hall Inc., Englewood Cliffs, N. J., 1966).

Some other relevant books and articles are:
38. Aaron, R. I.: *The Nature of Knowing* (Williams and Norgate, 1930).

39. Aaron, R. I.: 'Feeling Sure', *Proceedings of the Aristotelian Society*, Supplementary Volume XXX (1956), pp. 1–13.
40. Adams, E. M.: 'On Knowing That', *Philosophical Quarterly*, Vol. 8 (1958), pp. 300–306.
41. Armstrong, J. H. S.: 'Knowledge and Belief', *Analysis*, Vol. 13 (1952–3), pp. 111–117.
42. Arner, D.: 'On Knowing', *Philosophical Review*, Vol. LXVIII (1959), pp. 84–92.
43. Barnes, W. H. F.: 'Knowing', *Philosophical Review*, LXXII (1963), pp. 3–16.
44. Black, Max: 'Saying and Disbelieving', *Analysis*, Vol. 13, No. 2 (1952–3). Also in Max Black, *Problems of Analysis*, pp. 46–57 (Cornell U.P., Ithaca, N.Y., 1954).
45. Wilks, R.: 'Prof. Black on "Saying and Disbelieving"', *Analysis*, Vol. 14 (1953–4), pp. 24–5.
46. Braithwaite, R. B.: 'Belief and Action', *Proceedings of the Aristotelian Society*, Supplementary Volume XX (1946), pp. 1–19.
47. Carmichael, P. A.: 'Knowing', *Journal of Philosophy*, Vol. LVI (1959), pp. 341–351.
48. Chisholm, R.: 'Sentences about Believing', *Proceedings of the Aristotelian Society*, (1955–6), pp. 125–148.
49. Landesman, C.: 'A note on Belief', *Analysis*, Vol. 24 (1963–4), pp. 180–182.
50. Chisholm, R. M.: 'A note on Saying', *Analysis*, Vol. 24 (1963–4), pp. 182–4.
51. Chisholm, R. M.: 'The Logic of Knowing', *Journal of Philosophy*, Vol. LX (1963), pp. 773–795.
52. Firth, R.: 'Chisholm on the Ethics of Belief', *Philosophical Review*, Volume LXVIII (1959), pp. 493–506.
53. Deutscher, M.: 'A note on Saying and Disbelieving', *Analysis*, Vol. 25 (1964–5), pp. 13–17.
54. Bonney, W. L.: 'Mr. Deutscher on Saying and Disbelieving', *Analysis*, Vol. 25 (1964–5), pp. 17–20.
55. Grant, C. K.: 'Belief in and Belief That', *XIIth International Congress of Philosophy*, Vol. 5 (1959), pp. 187–194.
56. Hartland-Swann, J.: '"Being aware of" and "Knowing"', *Philosophical Quarterly*, Vol. 7 (1957), pp. 126–135.
57. Harrison, J.: 'Does Knowing imply Believing?', *Philosophical Quarterly*, Volume 13 (1963), pp. 322–332.
58. Hedelberger, H.: 'Knowledge, Certainty, and Probability', *Inquiry*, Vol. 6, (1963), pp. 242–250.

59. Lewis, C. I.: *Knowledge and Valuation* (Open Court, New York, 1946) (esp. the Introduction).

60. Mace, C. A.: 'Belief', *Proceedings of the Aristotelian Society*, Vol. XXIX, (1928–9), pp. 227–250.

61. MacIver, A. M.: 'Knowledge', *Proceedings of the Aristotelian Society*, Supplementary Volume XXXII (1958), pp. 1–24.

62. Martin, R. M.: 'On Knowing, Believing, Thinking', *Journal of Philosophy*, Vol. LIX (1962), pp. 586–600 (replied to by R. M. Anderson, ibid., pp. 600–607).

63. Murphree, Iris: 'Experimental Nature of Belief', *Journal of Philosophy*, Vol. LX, (1963) pp. 309–317.

64. Polanyi, M.: 'Knowing and Being', *Mind*, Vol. LXX, (1961), pp. 458–470.

65. Russell, L. J.: 'Two Ways of Knowing—by contemplating and by doing', *Indian Journal of Philosophy*, Vol. II (1961), pp. 83–95.

66. Schiller, F. C. S.: *Problems of Belief* (Doran & Co., New York, 1924).

67. Sesonske, A.: 'On Believing', *Journal of Philosophy*, Vol. LVI (1959), pp. 486–492.

68. Smullyan, A.: 'The Concept of Empirical Knowledge', *Philosophical Review*, Vol. LXV (1956).

69. Thomas, L. E.: 'Philosophic Doubt', *Mind*, Vol. LXIV (1955), pp. 333–341.

70. Wang, Hao: 'A Question on Knowledge of Knowledge', *Analysis*, Vol. 14 (1953–4), pp. 142–146.

71. Weiler, G.: 'Degrees of Knowledge', *Philosophical Quarterly*, Vol. XV (1965), pp. 317–327.

INDEX OF NAMES

(*not including authors mentioned only in the Bibliography*)